NASCAR
GREATEST RACES

THE 25 MOST THRILLING RACES IN NASCAR HISTORY

BY TOM HIGGINS

NASCAR
GREATEST RACES

THE 25 MOST THRILLING RACES IN NASCAR HISTORY

BY TOM HIGGINS

HarperEntertainment
A Division of HarperCollinsPublishers

www.harpercollins.com

A TEHABI BOOK

TEHABI BOOKS

NASCAR Greatest Races was conceived and produced by Tehabi Books. *Tehabi*—symbolizing the spirit of teamwork—derives its name from the Hopi Indian tribe of the southwestern United States. As an award-winning book producer, Tehabi works with national and international publishers, corporations, institutions, and nonprofit groups to identify, develop, and implement comprehensive publishing programs. Tehabi Books is located in Del Mar, California. www.tehabi.com

Chris Capen, *President*
Tom Lewis, *Editorial and Design Director*
Sharon Lewis, *Controller*
Nancy Cash, *Managing Editor*
Andy Lewis, *Senior Art Director*
Sarah Morgans, *Associate Editor*
Mo Latimer, *Editorial Assistant*
Maria Medina, *Administrative Assistant*
Kevin Giontzeneli, *Production Artist*
Curtis Boyer, *Production Artist*
Sam Lewis, *Webmaster*
Ross Eberman, *Director of Custom Publishing*
Tim Connolly, *Sales and Marketing Manager*
Eric Smith, *Marketing Assistant*
Tiffany Smith, *Executive Assistant*
Bill Center, *Developmental Editor*
Gail Fink, *Copy Editor*
Jeff Campbell, *Proofreader*

We would like to thank the panel of sportswriters for their efforts in compiling the race survey.
Bill Center
Mike Harris
Tom Higgins
Bob Moore

Tehabi Books offers special discounts for bulk purchases for sales promotions or premiums. Specific, large quantity needs can be met with special editions, including personalized covers, excerpts of existing materials, and corporate imprints. For more information, contact Tehabi Books, 1201 Camino Del Mar, Suite 100, Del Mar, CA 92014, (800) 243-7259.

HarperEntertainment
A Division of HarperCollinsPublishers

NASCAR Greatest Races was published by HarperEntertainment, a Division of HarperCollins Publishers Inc., 10 East 53rd Street, New York, NY 10022. www.harpercollins.com
John Silbersack, *Senior Vice President and Publishing Director*
Frank Fochetta, *Vice President and Director of HarperCollins Enterprises*
Amy Wasserman, *Marketing Director*
Susan Sanguily, *Creative Director*

With special thanks to key individuals at NASCAR for their contributions in the creation of *NASCAR Greatest Races*.
Kelly Crouch, *Director of Special Projects and Publishing*
Jennifer White, *Editorial Manager*
Paul Schaefer, *Senior Editor*
Fay Theos, *Executive Producer/NASCAR Online*

NASCAR is a registered trademark of the National Association for Stock Car Auto Racing, Inc. www.nascar.com

Photography credits appear on page 144.

Library of Congress Cataloging-in-Publication Data

Higgins, Tom, 1937–
     NASCAR greatest races : the 25 most thrilling races in NASCAR history / by Tom Higgins.
          p.   cm.
     "A Tehabi book."
     ISBN 0-06-105152-7
     1. Stock car racing—United States.   2. NASCAR (Association)
I. Title.
GV1029.9.S74H54   1999 fol.
796.72'0973—dc21   99-43464
                                                                          CIP

99 00 01 02 03 / TB 10 9 8 7 6 5 4 3 2 1

This edition is printed on acid-free paper that meets the American National Standards Institute Z39.48 standard.
Printed in the United States through R.R. Donnelley & Sons Company.

CONTENTS

Witnessing Great Ones

by Ned Jarrett

When you talk to NASCAR fans and sportswriters about the greatest races, you hear all of the same memories: watching with amused disbelief as the Allison brothers tussled with Cale Yarborough at the end of the 1979 Daytona 500; choking back a tear as rivals' crews lined pit row to high-five Dale Earnhardt after his long-awaited Daytona 500 win; feeling the swell of pride as Air Force One touched down at Daytona International Speedway in 1984 with President Reagan aboard. These were all very visual moments in a very visual spectator sport. They were about witnessing.

So when it was time to talk to NASCAR drivers about the races they felt were among the greatest, there was some concern that theirs would be an entirely different perspective. That the races deemed among the greatest by the participants would not jive with the spectators' picks. But that thinking proved wrong, and I think I know why.

I started my NASCAR driving career in the early 1950s in a 1937 Ford. My dad, who owned a farm and a sawmill, was not too happy about his son risking his life on the rugged dirt tracks and participating with that wild group of race drivers. But as time went by and he realized my love for the sport, my dad became my biggest fan. And those thirteen years as a NASCAR driver were pretty thrilling. Hitting milestones in a sport rife with possibilities, dueling with good-natured rivals, defying all odds by coming from behind, and ending a race with a fabulous finish were all experiences made possible by being the driver behind the wheel. But as a driver I still felt like I was witnessing the great moments as much as participating in them. And when I remember back to those times, I recall them with the same panning-the-track perspective that many spectators had.

Now, as an auto racing announcer, I get to witness NASCAR's great races from another perspective, straddling the lines between driver, journalist, and fan. Those lines are a lot blurrier than in most sports—the result, I think, of NASCAR's down-to-earth drivers, officials, and fans.

The greatest races laid out in this volume reflect the sentiments of everyone who has made NASCAR what it is. Hundreds of fans and sportswriters and dozens of the top drivers gave us their picks for the cream of NASCAR's crop. In all likelihood you will find the races you consider great in the following pages. But if a race you consider particularly important is absent from this book, you can pan across the track in your mind's eye and know that that's the way the participating driver is probably thinking of it, too.

Firsts &

Milestones

The races that ushered in new eras and raised the bar for racing

1948
Rayson Memorial

"Although Red won the race for the third straight year, I know this one became special to him because he was the
first driver to ever win a NASCAR race."

—RAYMOND PARKS, WHO OWNED RED BYRON'S 1939 FORD COUPE
AND STARTED THE FORD THAT BOB FLOCK DROVE TO A THIRD-PLACE FINISH

It was the one that started it all. And it wasn't a bad race, either.

William H. G. "Big Bill" France had only months earlier founded the National Association for Stock Car Auto Racing at the Streamline Hotel in Daytona Beach, Florida. France had conceived the sanctioning organization out of frustration over the mismanagement and general shadiness of auto racing. So he called and chaired a meeting of thirty-five other promoters to establish bylaws and rules.

France brimmed with optimism as race day neared in the winter of 1948. The course location had been moved southward to the combination Beach-Road Course on the shore of the Atlantic Ocean at Ponce Inlet. Booming postwar construction in the Daytona Beach area had necessitated relocation.

"The turns of our new 2.2-mile course are something to see," said France. "There won't be any dull moments when the boys come roaring through that south turn, especially. It's a corker."

Also boosting France's confidence was the receipt of sixty-two entries from twelve states.

"We expect at least fifty drivers to show up with cars and race," he said.

Drivers Ed Samples (far left) and Fonty Flock stand alongside the Rayson Memorial trophy with famed driver E. G. "Cannonball" Baker and NASCAR founder Bill France Sr. before the start of NASCAR's first sanctioned race on the historic Beach-Road Course.

Red Byron wins NASCAR's

first sanctioned race

"The drivers were all interested to see if NASCAR was going to be better than what we had. There had been promises before. **I always thought this was one of the greatest days in stock car history."**

—DRIVER TIM FLOCK

The Rayson Memorial trophy was dedicated in 1945 with the provision that it would become the property of the first driver to win the race three times. After Ray Hall won the inaugural, Red Byron, considered the best stock car racer of the immediate post–World War II era, won three straight Rayson Memorials, with the third victory coming in NASCAR's first sanctioned race in 1948. Byron went on to become NASCAR's first and second season champion.

It turned out that fifty-six drivers took the green flag on a track comprised almost equally of hard-packed sand along the beach and a long, straight stretch of U.S. A1A. A crowd estimated at fourteen thousand, paying $2.50 each, showed up to watch the sixty-eight-lap, 149.6-mile event. A story in a local newspaper declared that spectators "were thicker than the seeds on rye bread."

Fearing a pileup during the early laps, France and other officials decided on a staggered start. Each row of cars was sent off at an interval of one second. Several drivers exited via accidents in the tricky south turn, barely missing a creaky observation tower full of nervous officials. But local hero Marshall Teague stayed in the race and charged from the front row to lead the first lap of NASCAR competition. On lap thirty-five, colorful Fonty Flock caught up to Teague entering the hairpin north turn and took the lead. However, while running a half mile ahead on lap fifty, Flock's car broke a spindle and sailed off the course and out of the race.

Teague was the leader again, but his brakes were failing and Red Byron was closing in. The two caught a slower moving car in the north turn. Teague maneuvered to the inside. Byron, maintaining momentum, swept outside and emerged from the corner thirty yards ahead. Now the trick was to stay in the race. The increasing choppiness of the north turn left only twelve starters on the track at the finish. Byron stayed in front of them the rest of the way, finishing fifteen seconds ahead of runner-up Teague for a third straight Daytona Beach victory.

"You can't win a horse race without a good horse, and you can't win a car race without a good car," said Byron, crediting famed mechanic Red Vogt for fielding the winning 1939 Ford Coupe. "Red puts his motors together like a fine watch. He's the reason I win."

But local news reports were more intrigued by Byron than his car. One story noted Byron's war injuries and the adjustments made to accommodate them. "Byron was wearing a steel stirrup on his left leg, smashed by Japanese flak in World War II. The injury also requires having his left shoe belted to a special clutch."

Among those taking part who'd later gain NASCAR fame were Raymond Parks, Buddy Shuman, Fireball Roberts, Curtis Turner, Jim Paschal, Buck Baker, and Bob and Tim Flock.

Fonty Flock was leading the Rayson Memorial by almost a half mile on the fiftieth lap when the front spindle on his 1939 Ford Coupe broke, causing him to roll three times and wind up in the bushes. Flock was uninjured but his race was over.

1948 RAYSON MEMORIAL
FEBRUARY 15, 1948
DAYTONA BEACH, FLORIDA
2.2-MILE BEACH-ROAD COURSE

Place	Driver	Make	Laps	Money	Pole Pos.
1.	Red Byron	Ford	68	$1,000	NA
2.	Marshall Teague	Ford	68	$650	NA
3.	Bob Flock*	Ford	68	$450	NA
4.	Buddy Shuman	Ford	68	$300	NA
5.	Wayne Pritchett	Ford	68	$200	NA
6.	J. L. McMichaels	Ford	67	$150	NA
7.	Lee Morgan	Ford	67	$100	NA
8.	Ed Samples	Ford	66	$50	NA
9.	Howard Farmer	Ford	65	$50	NA
10.	Johnny Grubb	Ford	65	$50	NA

*Drove in relief of Raymond Parks

Time of Race: 1 hour, 58 minutes, 30 seconds
Average Speed: 75.747 mph
Margin of Victory: 15 seconds
Pole Winner: No time trials

1959
Daytona 500

". . . looking at Daytona for the first time was stunning.
We had never seen anything like the banking and that long back straight." —GLEN WOOD

The 1959 Daytona 500 proved momentous in so many ways. It was the first of the classic NASCAR Winston Cup Series races and the first race to be held at Bill France Sr.'s never-before-tested 2.5-mile high-banked track. It also ushered in one of the most nerve-racking aspects of the sport: the photo finish.

Lee Petty and Johnny Beauchamp swept to the checkered flag side by side in the inaugural Daytona 500, forging a finish that initially proved too close to call correctly. Complicating matters at the sprawling, newly opened Daytona International Speedway was the lapped car of Joe Weatherly, running alongside the leaders.

As the pack neared the finish line, NASCAR founder/president Bill France Sr. peered down from a position at the base of the flag stand and declared that Beauchamp had won. Top NASCAR aide John Bruner agreed. But protests immediately arose from Petty and his crewmen, plus members of the media and fans whose vantage points provided a view of the stripe. Their contention was that Petty had prevailed by a foot or so.

Beauchamp went to victory lane. He first said, "I

Lee Petty's Oldsmobile (42) leads Johnny Beauchamp's Thunderbird (73) to the finish line in one of the pictures used to determine the winner of the first race at Daytona International Speedway. Not only was the finish close, the judges' view was partially blocked by the lapped car of Joe Weatherly (on the high side in car 48).

First Annual
Official Souvenir Program
NASCAR SANCTIONED
500 MILE
INTERNATIONAL SWEEPSTAKES
AND OTHER RACING EVENTS
FEB. 20, 21, 22, 1959

10th Annual
Safety and
Performance Trials
Feb. 15-16, 1959

PRICE
$1.00

Daytona International Speedway
"WORLD'S FASTEST AND FINEST RACE COURSE"
DAYTONA BEACH, FLORIDA

First photo finish: Lee Petty

9

GREATEST RACES

"What people forgot about the first Daytona 500, because of the finish, was that Fireball [Roberts] went **from forty-sixth to first in twenty-three laps** and was running away when his fuel pump broke."

—DRIVER ELMO LANGLEY

wins inaugural Daytona 500

1959 DAYTONA 500
FEBRUARY 22, 1959
DAYTONA INTERNATIONAL SPEEDWAY
DAYTONA BEACH, FLORIDA
2.5-MILE BANKED TRI-OVAL SUPERSPEEDWAY

Place	Driver	Make	Laps	Money	Pole Pos.
1.	Lee Petty	Olds.	200	$19,050	15
2.	Johnny Beauchamp	Ford	200	$7,650	21
3.	Charley Griffith	Pont.	199	$4,600	17
4.	Cotton Owens	Pont.	199	$2,525	11
5.	Joe Weatherly	Chev.	199	$1,875	7
6.	Jim Reed	Chev.	196	$1,075	39
7.	Jack Smith	Chev.	196	$2,625	41
8.	Tom Pistone	Ford	195	$1,825	5
9.	Tim Flock	Ford	193	$800	42
10.	Speedy Thompson	Chev.	193	$600	31

Time of Race:	3 hours, 41 minutes, 22 seconds
Average Speed:	135.521 mph
Margin of Victory:	2 feet
Pole Winner:	Bob Welborn, Chev., 140.121 mph
Fastest Qualifier:	Cotton Owens, 143.196 mph

hope I won . . . I don't know." Then he said, "I beat him about that far," and held his hands a foot apart. "I could just glimpse his front bumper when we crossed the line."

Meanwhile, controversy and uncertainty continued to swirl. After six hours of discussion, France fairly and manfully ordered the race's outcome considered unofficial until photographs and movies of the seeming dead-heat could be studied.

"From where John Bruner and I stood it appeared Beauchamp edged Petty a little and won the race. But the track has a slight curve at that point, so we couldn't be positive," said France, who could have had trouble distinguishing among the cars of Beauchamp, Petty, and Weatherly, which were all painted white. "So we're going to look at a lot of pictures before deciding who won."

Film poured into NASCAR headquarters in Daytona Beach from all over the country, including a reel from Hearst Metrotone News in New York. Every shot showed stock car racing pioneer Petty slightly ahead. Throughout the wait, Petty, who would claim his third NASCAR points championship in 1959, insisted he wasn't worried the correct decision would be made. "I'm sleeping good," said Petty. "'Cause I know I had Beauchamp beat by about two feet."

Approximately sixty-two hours after the checkered flag had waved, France declared Petty the winner. France said that NASCAR would never be placed in such a difficult position again at Daytona.

"This is the first time so close a finish has ever occurred in auto racing," he stated. "We won't be caught off guard again. We'll install a photo finish camera at the line."

One thing NASCAR officials had been on guard about was the potential for accidents at the 2.5-mile high-banked track born of France's expansive imagination. There had been concern about the drivers racing on so large a speedway for the first time at speeds they'd never experienced, but there wasn't a single accident despite strong competition that produced thirty-three lead changes. In running the two-hundred-lap event without a caution period, Petty averaged 135.521 mph.

Petty assessed the remarkable race for a reporter with a telling comment:

"If you can't write about this," the crafty North Carolinian drawled, "you can't write about nothing."

Johnny Beauchamp, opposite, is awarded the winner's trophy after the inaugural Daytona 500. It was later awarded, below, to Lee Petty (right) by Bill France Sr. after finish-line photos showed Petty ahead of Beauchamp. Bottom: Petty's son Richard drove a convertible in the race but only lasted eight laps.

1985
Southern 500

"It was incredible the way it worked out. I'm sure Winston looked at history and saw how hard it was for anyone to win three of the four majors when they set up the program. Then **Bill goes right out and claims the prize** *in the first year."*

—HARRY MELLING, OWNER OF BILL ELLIOTT'S FORD, ON WINNING THE WINSTON MILLION

It was the richest prize in motorsports, and it was within Bill Elliott's reach. He could be the first to win the Winston Million, a prize offered for the first time that 1985 season. To win, a driver had to win three of the four major races on the NASCAR Winston Cup Series—the Daytona 500, the Winston 500 at Talladega, the World 600 at Charlotte, and the Southern 500 at Darlington. Earlier victories in the Daytona and Winston 500s gave Elliott two of the three necessary triumphs, setting him up to take the prize in Charlotte's World 600. But a variety of mechanical problems landed him twenty-one laps behind winner Darrell Waltrip at the finish, causing the $1 million prize to elude him.

Now it was Bill Elliott's final chance.

"I shut my eyes," Elliott said of the many near misses he experienced in the wreck-filled 367-lap race. "This is the toughest race I've ever run. I thought it never was going to end."

During the middle of the race Elliott endured a handling problem that became so bad that his tires started to blister. A timely caution flag enabled his crew to

Bill Elliott averts catastrophe to

NASCAR
12
GREATEST RACES

Second-fastest qualifier David Pearson (21) had a slight lead on pole-sitter Bill Elliott (9) in a battle of the Fords early in the 1985 Southern 500.

become first Winston Millionaire

remove a frayed tire that likely wouldn't have lasted another lap.

But the scariest incident and the one that threatened to cost Elliott the prize occurred on lap 319. Strong-running Dale Earnhardt, who had dominated along with Harry Gant, spun directly in front of Elliott coming off the second turn. Earnhardt hit the outer wall, then angled across the track. By opting to go to the apron, Elliott missed a hard collision by inches.

Minutes later, on the 324th lap, leader Cale Yarborough's car emitted a rooster tail of thick smoke in turn four. Elliott, only a car-length behind, was essentially blinded. Yarborough's problem was a broken power steering line. Fluid covered Elliott's car, but none got onto his tires. If some had, it could have caused a loss of control. Elliott again whipped to the apron and got by.

"Honestly, I'm surprised I didn't wreck both times," said Elliott, shaking his head. "I don't know why I didn't. I'm sure I had my eyes closed."

Yarborough somehow kept going straight and made it to his pit where the belt on the power steering pump was cut. Yarborough returned to the track without losing a lap to mount a strong challenge to Elliott. Yarborough dogged Elliott over the closing laps, trying to take the storied Southern 500 for the sixth time.

"It steered like a freight train. It took both arms, both hands, and both legs to turn that thing," said Yarborough of his Ford.

"But even that wasn't enough to get back around Bill."

In the end, Elliott escaped all of these potential catastrophes—spewing fluid and evading his rivals' spins—as if charmed. Elliott flashed across the finish line six-tenths of a second ahead of runner-up Yarborough. The popular victory set off a wild celebration among seventy thousand fans. In victory lane, commemorative $1 million bills bearing the face of Elliott were poured onto the head of the grinning winner.

"Awesome Bill" was now "Million Dollar Bill."

Bill Elliott (9) leads runner-up Cale Yarborough (28) coming off turn four in the closing moments of the 1985 Southern 500, below. Left: Elliott's crew performs a flawless pit stop.

"Every once in awhile, there's a car-driver combination that becomes the ticket on the big tracks. 1985 belonged to Bill Elliott."

—CALE YARBOROUGH

1985 SOUTHERN 500
SEPTEMBER 1, 1985
DARLINGTON RACEWAY
DARLINGTON, SOUTH CAROLINA
1.366-MILE EGG-SHAPED SUPERSPEEDWAY

Place	Driver	Make	Laps	Money	Pole Pos.
1.	Bill Elliott	Ford	367	$53,725*	1
2.	Cale Yarborough	Ford	367	$22,050	22
3.	Geoffrey Bodine	Chev.	367	$21,975	17
4.	Neil Bonnett	Chev.	366	$17,425	21
5.	Ron Bouchard	Buick	366	$13,330	19
6.	Ricky Rudd	Ford	366	$13,450	11
7.	Terry Labonte	Chev.	365	$15,500	9
8.	Benny Parsons	Chev.	365	$5,800	3
9.	Joe Ruttman	Chev.	364	$5,350	4
10.	Kyle Petty	Ford	364	$9,995	25

*Plus $1 million Winston Million prize

Time of Race:	4 hours, 8 minutes, 2 seconds
Average Speed:	121.254 mph
Margin of Victory:	0.6 second
Pole Winner:	Bill Elliott, 156.641 mph

*T*he battle between the Fords of Bill Elliott (9) and Cale Yarborough (28), right, included one scary moment on the 324th lap when Yarborough's car ruptured a power steering line while leading, below. Elliott was running a close second at the time and although his car was coated with the fluid, he ducked to the inside to take the lead.

Bill Elliott and the Melling Racing Team celebrate the Winston Million, below right. Elliott won at Daytona, Talladega, and Darlington.

"A lot of things you remember in racing are the accidents you couldn't avoid. One of my biggest memories from the 1985 Southern 500 was the number of times we didn't crash when something happened right in front of us."

—Bill Elliott

Winston Million

To: *Bill Elliott*   **$1,000,000**

ONE MILLION DOLLARS

1949

Strictly Stock Race No. 1

"After the race, I was just sitting there thinking about having to go home and **explain to my wife where I'd been with the car."**

—Lee Petty, who drove the family's Buick from Level Cross, North Carolina, to compete in NASCAR's first Strictly Stock race then rolled the car on the 107th lap

The most popular form of stock car racing when Bill France Sr. formed NASCAR in 1948 was the Modified class, which was the only division NASCAR sanctioned in its first season. But France believed that for stock car racing to become popular, the races had to be staged in cars driven by the general public.

On June 19, 1949, on a three-quarter-mile dirt track at Charlotte, North Carolina, France launched his Strictly Stock class—the predecessor to what became the Grand National and eventually the mega-popular NASCAR Winston Cup Series.

Although the first Strictly Stock race wasn't announced until the spring of 1949, the event attracted thirty-three drivers and nine different makes of cars—Lincoln, Hudson, Ford, Oldsmobile, Cadillac, Buick, Chrysler, Kaiser, and Mercury. When slightly more than thirteen thousand spectators paid to see the event, France knew he had a winner.

The only modification allowed from stock was a metal plate on the outside of the right front wheel to prevent the lug nuts from wearing through the metal wheel.

At the race's start, the Flock brothers of Atlanta, Georgia, had the early edge. Bob Flock won the pole with a fast lap of 67.958 mph in a 1946 Hudson. Outside him on the front row was Tim Flock in a 1949 Olds 88. And on the inside of the third row was Fonty Flock in a '49 Hudson.

But the dominant car was a 1947 Ford driven by Glenn Dunnaway, which took the checkered flag on the two-hundredth lap with a three-lap lead on the 1949 Lincoln that Jim Roper had driven all the way from Great Bend, Kansas, after reading about the race in the popular "Smilin' Jack" comic strip.

But Major Al Crisler, NASCAR's first technical inspector, discovered that Dunnaway's car, which was owned and qualified by Hubert Westmoreland, had nonstock "altered rear springs" that gave the Ford far better stability in the rutted turns. Dunnaway was disqualified and Roper was declared the winner.

Westmoreland sued, but the case was thrown out of court. NASCAR, it was judged, had the right to set rules for its races—which was a major victory for the still-fledgling sanctioning body.

Based on the success of the Charlotte race, France scheduled nine more Strictly Stock races in 1949. The following year, he renamed the division Grand National and put it ahead of the Modifieds as No. 1 in the NASCAR lineup. The rest is history.

Inaugural Strictly

1948 NASCAR champion Red Byron (22)
moves his 1949 Oldsmobile to the inside of
Otis Martin's 1948 Ford (19) early in
NASCAR's first Strictly Stock race. Opposite:
Ticket prices ranged from $2 to $4.

1949 STRICTLY STOCK RACE NO. 1
CHARLOTTE SPEEDWAY
CHARLOTTE, NORTH CAROLINA
3/4-MILE DIRT OVAL

Place	Driver	Make	Laps	Money	Pole Pos.
1.	Jim Roper	Lincln.	197	$2,000	12
2.	Fonty Flock	Hudsn.	197	$1,000	5
3.	Red Byron	Olds.	197	$500	3
4.	Sam Rice	Olds.	197	$300	14
5.	Tim Flock	Olds.	197	$200	2

Because Roper was awarded the victory after
Glenn Dunnaway was disqualified, there was no
posted average speed or margin of victory.
Pole winner: Bob Flock, Hudson, 67.958 mph

150-Mile National Championship STRICTLY **Stock Car Race**

SUNDAY, JUNE 19th SANCTIONED BY N.A.S.C.A.R. **$5,000 Purse**
200 LAPS

★ **CHARLOTTE SPEEDWAY** ★
Beautiful Banked Three-Quarter-Mile Speedway — Another Bill France Classic
OPEN TO 1946-47-48-49 AMERICAN-MADE CARS ONLY —
FOR ENTRY BLANKS OR INFORMATION WRITE OR WIRE - BILL FRANCE, 614 S. ELM ST., GREENSBORO, N. C.
ADMISSION INCLUDING TAX $2, $3, $4

Stock Race decided by rules

1984
Pepsi Firecracker 400

"I'd been waiting for number two hundred for an awfully long time. But it was worth the wait, the way it happened with the president being there and on July 4.
I couldn't have asked for a better time." —RICHARD PETTY

It was the only time a county commissioner ever upstaged the president of the United States. President Ronald Reagan, the first sitting U.S. president to attend an auto race, was among those watching the drama of the 1984 Firecracker 400. But that milestone event was eclipsed by the even greater milestone reached by the driver known as "The King."

Driver Richard Petty, who sat as a county commissioner back home in Level Cross, North Carolina, went into the race with 199 NASCAR Winston Cup Series wins under his belt. After President Reagan gave the field the command to start engines via radio from Air Force One ninety minutes before landing just beyond turn two, Petty and Cale Yarborough led the pack.

After the last series of pit stops, Petty and Yarborough dueled for the lead as they thundered to a twenty-five-second advantage over the field. With 20 of the 160 laps remaining on the 2.5-mile track, they were locked in a close two-car draft. Petty was leading with Yarborough in second place, positioned for an aerodynamic slingshot pass, a move he had made to win the two most recent Daytona 500s.

Petty and Yarborough each made feinting moves, feeling each other out for what loomed as a last-lap shootout. But at the start of

The King takes two-hundredth

Richard Petty's Pontiac flies down the track with Air Force One in the 1984 Firecracker 400 at Daytona International Speedway.

in front of the president

1984 PEPSI FIRECRACKER 400 JULY 4, 1984 DAYTONA INTERNATIONAL SPEEDWAY DAYTONA BEACH, FLORIDA 2.5-MILE BANKED TRI-OVAL SUPERSPEEDWAY				
Place Driver	**Make**	**Laps**	**Money**	**Pole Pos.**
1. Richard Petty	Pont.	160	$43,755	6
2. Harry Gant	Chev.	160	$26,570	13
3. Cale Yarborough	Chev.	160	$23,640	1
4. Bobby Allison	Buick	160	$21,850	10
5. Benny Parsons	Chev.	160	$10,450	9
6. Bill Elliott	Ford	160	$14,050	3
7. Terry Labonte	Chev.	159	$11,975	4
8. Dale Earnhardt	Chev.	159	$13,500	2
9. Neil Bonnett	Chev.	159	$7,995	19
10. Joe Ruttman	Chev.	157	$9,255	18

Time of Race:	2 hours, 19 minutes, 59 seconds
Average Speed:	171.204 mph
Margin of Victory:	Under caution
Pole Winner:	Cale Yarborough, 199.743 mph

"I was so happy for him. It was almost like someone had written the perfect story for The King.

Everything came together today for my dad and the sport."

—KYLE PETTY

the 158th lap, rookie Doug Heveron's car bobbled and flipped onto the grassy apron in turn one. Heveron wasn't hurt, but the accident forced a yellow flag. It was obvious the race was going to end under caution.

Petty and Yarborough had passed the flag stand when the yellow waved, so whichever driver got back to the line first was virtually assured of victory. Racing back is permitted for those who haven't taken the yellow.

Yarborough made his move on the backstretch, slingshotting past Petty's famed No. 43 in turn three. However, Petty immediately moved to the inside and drew abreast in turn four. The cars seemed melded as they hurtled through the tri-oval portion of the track leading to the line. As they drifted apart by perhaps a foot, Petty seemed to surge ahead slightly.

"We touched real hard three or four times," said Petty, who had celebrated his forty-seventh birthday two days earlier. "The last 'bam' sort of squirted me ahead, giving me the slightest edge."

That was the race, although two laps remained to be run at reduced speed. Obviously swept up by the excitement, Yarborough thought the show was over and drove down pit road on the 159th lap. Realizing his error, Cale sped back onto the track in his Chevrolet, but the lapse cost him second place. Harry Gant, almost a half lap behind when the yellow flew, had gone by to take the position.

A euphoric Petty stopped his winning Pontiac at the finish line after taking a cooldown lap and was escorted quickly to the tower suite of NASCAR president Bill France Jr. to meet with President Reagan.

"Were you and Cale actually touching fenders coming down the stretch?" the president asked incredulously.

"Yes sir, we were," replied an honored Petty, who later revealed, "It [blew] the president's mind that me and Cale were hitting each other at two hundred miles an hour."

Yarborough's error created perhaps the greatest trivia question in NASCAR history: Who finished second in the 1984 Firecracker 400?

"My brain blew up, I guess," explained Yarborough. "I flat messed up. . . . But I'm glad to see Richard get his two-hundredth. Now he can start on three hundred."

That wasn't to be. Petty continued to drive through the 1992 season before retiring, but never again won after the triumph that earned his car a place in the Smithsonian Institution.

Richard Petty accepts the checkered flag on his record two-hundredth NASCAR Winston Cup victory while cruising behind the pace car under the caution flag, opposite.

Below: President Ronald Reagan receives the Firecracker 400 checkered flag from winner Richard Petty (right) and Bobby Allison during postrace ceremonies. The flag was signed by all forty-two drivers who competed that day.

1994 Brickyard 400

"With every lap, you feel the history and the tradition. The shadows from the stands, the four distinct turns, and the vastness of the place. To a racer, this is nirvana."

—Darrell Waltrip

It was the home of the venerable racetrack that had been around since the first years of the century. It was also the hometown of a young driver who had just garnered his first victory in the NASCAR Winston Cup Series. Jeff Gordon made the inaugural Brickyard 400 at the fabled Indianapolis Motor Speedway a storybook spectacular—one that was spiced by a family feud.

Gordon, who grew up in nearby Pittsboro and turned twenty-three just forty-eight hours before the race, thrilled a partisan, provincial crowd estimated at three hundred thousand, a record for the NASCAR Winston Cup Series. A flat right front tire forced Ernie Irvan to fall off the pace while leading and pit on the 156th of 160 laps at the world-famous 2.5-mile track, where no race other than the Indianapolis 500 had been staged before. Until the tire problem, Irvan and Gordon had either raced abreast or bumper-to-bumper for twenty laps, exchanging the lead five times. They alternately nosed front bumpers under each other's rear deck spoilers, affecting the slipstream airflow to make the leading car "loose," or slip sideways.

"We had a mind game going on," said Irvan, who dropped back to finish seventeenth. "From where I was at, I thought I was going to beat Jeff. And from where he was at, I'm sure he thought he was going to beat me. It was great racing. I think the fans got a terrific show."

NASCAR hits the bricks:

Jeff Gordon, who moved to the Indianapolis area as a teenager to launch his driving career, celebrates after his win in the inaugural Brickyard 400 at the Indianapolis Motor Speedway.

Indianapolis Motor Speedway

"I never imagined this could happen. Before, when you made a choice to race stock cars, it meant you weren't going to run at this fabulous place.

Now we're living in the best of both worlds."

—RUSTY WALLACE

"Me and Ernie were really working on each other," said Gordon. "I drove as hard as I could to make his car loose and get a run on him. If he hadn't had the flat, we probably would have come across the finish line side-by-side and Lord knows who would have won. Our cars were very equal."

The strongest car appeared to be that of Geoffrey Bodine, who led impressively until the 101st lap when he wrecked as the result of a tap from younger brother Brett. Brett had been bumped from the lead seconds earlier by Geoffrey.

"When Geoffrey went out, I thought all I'd have to do was be real smooth and cool the rest of the way and the race was mine," said Gordon, who narrowly missed the spinning car of Geoffrey Bodine. "Then here came Ernie." The race's sixth caution flag, showing on the 131st lap, enabled Irvan and a pack of other veterans to close in on their youthful rival. Gordon and Irvan steadily put some distance on the others, and the best battling of the race ensued on the track.

After Irvan slowed, Gordon coolly concentrated on maintaining his advantage over Brett Bodine, who surprisingly took second place despite bypassing extensive prerace testing at the speedway.

"Oh, my God! I did it! I did it!" Gordon shouted to his Hendrick Motorsports crew via radio as he got the checkered flag.

It was the second NASCAR Winston Cup Series victory for Gordon, a phenom as a teenager in open cockpit cars in the Midwest. His breakthrough win came in another major race, the Coca-Cola 600, a few weeks earlier on May 29, the same day as the Indy 500. Gordon had bawled like a baby in victory lane at Charlotte, but he was more composed at the speedway known as The Brickyard— even though he'd just earned a NASCAR single-race record of $613,000.

"Charlotte prepared me to deal with my emotion," said Gordon. "This time I took an extra victory lap to wipe the tears from my eyes."

Jeff Gordon moves past pole-sitter Rick Mast to gain his first lead in the Brickyard 400, opposite. Following are Geoffrey Bodine, Bobby Labonte, Bill Elliott, and Ricky Rudd. Below: A tired but happy A. J. Foyt climbs from his Ford. The first four-time winner of the Indy 500 came out of retirement to race in the inaugural NASCAR Winston Cup stock car race and finished thirteenth at the track that made him famous.

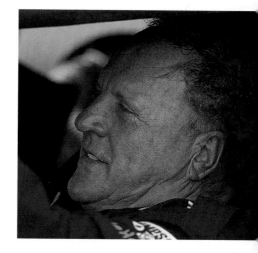

"This is the No. 1 place in the world. For NASCAR to be here shows how great a series it has become. I wanted to be here in this race.

I think this is fantastic for the speedway and NASCAR."

—A. J. FOYT

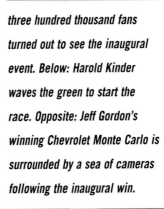

S Since it opened in 1911, the Indianapolis Motor Speedway had hosted one race a year— the Indianapolis 500 for open- wheel championship cars. All that changed in 1994 with the first running of the Brickyard 400. But the Indy tradition had plenty of room for the NASCAR Winston Cup family. Above: As seen beyond Rusty Wallace's pit stall, more than three hundred thousand fans turned out to see the inaugural event. Below: Harold Kinder waves the green to start the race. Opposite: Jeff Gordon's winning Chevrolet Monte Carlo is surrounded by a sea of cameras following the inaugural win.

1994 BRICKYARD 400
AUGUST 6, 1994
INDIANAPOLIS MOTOR SPEEDWAY
INDIANAPOLIS, INDIANA
2.5-MILE OVAL

Place	Driver	Make	Laps	Money	Pole Pos.
1.	Jeff Gordon	Chev.	160	$613,000	3
2.	Brett Bodine	Ford	160	$203,575	7
3.	Bill Elliott	Ford	160	$164,850	6
4.	Rusty Wallace	Ford	160	$140,600	12
5.	Dale Earnhardt	Chev.	160	$121,625	2
6.	Darrell Waltrip	Chev.	160	$82,600	27
7.	Ken Schrader	Chev.	160	$77,400	23
8.	Michael Waltrip	Pont.	160	$72,300	15
9.	Todd Bodine	Ford	160	$63,600	25
10.	Morgan Shepherd	Ford	160	$67,350	11

Time of Race:	3 hours, 1 minute, 59 seconds
Average Speed:	131.977 mph
Margin of Victory:	.53-second
Pole Winner:	Rick Mast, Ford, 172.414 mph

1950 Southern 500

"Everyone learned something
from Johnny Mantz in that first Darlington race."

—COTTON OWENS, DRIVER

Harold Brasington was a dreamer and a schemer who had a love for auto racing and for a legendary place called the Indianapolis Motor Speedway.

As NASCAR was gaining a foothold in stock car racing, Brasington went to work on his dream of re-creating Indiana's famed Brickyard in a field just outside the small South Carolina town of Darlington. Brasington's plan was to build a four-turn, 1.5-mile oval. But the necessity to avoid a fishing pond in one corner of the project turned the track into a 1.25-mile track with different radius turns at both ends.

Unknowingly, Brasington had created what would become NASCAR's first superspeedway and a track that is a vital part of the American racing experience.

"No place challenges a car and driver like Darlington," said Cale Yarborough, who snuck under the fence on September 4, 1950, to witness the first Southern 500—which was also NASCAR's first five-hundred-mile race.

In 1950, the idea of racing five hundred miles on asphalt was new to stock car racers used to running one-hundred-milers on dirt ovals. Enter Johnny Mantz, who campaigned Indianapolis 500-style cars out of Long Beach, California.

Mantz was entered in the inaugural Southern 500 in a Plymouth co-owned by NASCAR founder Bill France Sr., NASCAR official Alvin Hawkins, and mechanic Hubert Westmoreland. But it was the knowledge that Mantz brought from his Indy-car racing that carried the day. Mantz knew that the tires NASCAR's Grand National drivers were used to running on dirt tracks would not hold up on asphalt. So he ordered hard-compound truck tires like those used by Indianapolis 500 drivers.

Among the seventy-five cars that qualified for the first Southern 500, Mantz was the slowest at 73.460 mph—almost 9 mph below the pole-winning 82.034 mph posted by Curtis Turner's Oldsmobile.

But Mantz's Plymouth kept moving on the track while everyone else made countless stops for fresh rubber. Red Byron, for example, went through twenty-four tires before finishing third.

Mantz won by nine laps with an average speed of 75.250 mph, which was faster than his qualifying speed.

Truck tires help

In the front row of the three-abreast start of the inaugural Southern 500 were Gober Sosebee's 1950 Olds (51), Jimmy Thompson's 1950 Lincoln (25), and pole-sitter Curtis Turner's 1950 Olds.

1950 SOUTHERN 500
DARLINGTON RACEWAY
DARLINGTON, SOUTH CAROLINA
1.25-MILE BANKED OVAL

Place	Driver	Make	Laps	Money	Pole Pos.
1.	Johnny Mantz	Plymt.	400	$10,510	43
2.	Fireball Roberts	Olds.	391	$3,500	67
3.	Red Byron	Cad.	390	$2,000	7
4.	Bill Rexford	Olds.	385	$1,500	7
5.	Chuck Maloney	Merc.	381	$1,000	23
					15

Time of Race:	6 hours, 38 minutes, 40 seconds
Average Speed:	75.250 mph
Margin of Victory:	9-plus laps
Pole Winner:	Curtis Turner, Olds., 82.034 mph

Johnny Mantz poses with the Southern 500 hardware after winning by nine laps in his 1950 Plymouth shod with truck tires.

Mantz win at first superspeedway

Classic

Duels

The mano-a-mano matchups that thrilled fans and made memories

1984
Winston 500

"It was the wildest race I've ever been in.
Every time I got the lead, I immediately got shuffled back into the pack."

—Benny Parsons

Drivers Cale Yarborough and Harry Gant were each known for their hard-as-nails toughness. Both drivers, less than a year apart in age, would invariably battle each race out to the end in fearless form. But while Yarborough drove his first race as an underage entrant at Darlington Raceway, Gant started off his NASCAR Winston Cup Series career as a thirty-nine-year-old rookie. At the 1984 Winston 500 the two middle-aged heroes met, clashing on NASCAR's biggest, fastest track for the most competitive chase in the sanctioning body's history.

From the beginning the Winston 500 was thrilling. Counted only at the start/finish line on a lap-by-lap basis, there were seventy-five lead changes among thirteen drivers.

"It was amazing out there," said Yarborough, shaking his head, eyes flashing. "One second you'd be running first, then a couple seconds later a bunch of 'em drafted around and you'd be running tenth."

Going into the last lap, Yarborough was running out of fuel and barely trailing. But the determined, onrushing South Carolinian used the aerodynamics that come into play at high speed for a pivotal slingshot pass of leader Gant on the backstretch at Alabama International Motor Speedway. Gant tried to retaliate with a similar move on Yarborough through the tri-oval homestretch, but a lapped, slower car blocked the way.

Yarborough gets edge after

Each driver pictured in this midrace scramble was among the thirteen drivers who swapped the lead a record seventy-five times during the 1984 Winston 500 at Talladega. Richard Petty (43) is challenged by Dale Earnhardt (3) as eventual winner Cale Yarborough and Bobby Allison ride in Earnhardt's draft. To the inside are Buddy Baker (21) and Bill Elliott (9).

seventy-five lead changes

"It was an interesting race because the speeds were way up there, but not a lot of people made mistakes. There were only a couple of accidents, but a lot of equipment expired along the way."

—BOBBY ALLISON

"I barely made it to the finish line. . . . I was running on fumes," said a beaming Yarborough. "The motor started missing coming out of the fourth turn. I pumped the accelerator and jiggled the car from side to side to get the last little bit of gas into the carburetor. Any further and Harry very likely would have beat me.

"Also, if that slow car hadn't come into play through the track's dogleg, I'm sure Harry would have made it much closer," conceded Yarborough.

Gant trailed by two car lengths in finishing second for the fifteenth time in his career. Said Gant, "Cale is a tough competitor, so I don't know if I could have gotten back by him. I'd sure have liked a clear shot, but traffic is part of racing and it was nobody's fault."

Behind Yarborough and Gant there was a dandy duel for third place as Buddy Baker, Bobby Allison, and Benny Parsons crossed the line abreast. They were listed as finishing in that order after officials carefully studied photographs. Yarborough averaged 172.988 mph, an event record, in completing the five hundred miles in just two hours, fifty-three minutes, and twenty-seven seconds.

Cale Yarborough (28) angles his car out on pit row for a fast exit, opposite. Below: Yarborough is all smiles after his second Winston 500 victory.

1984 WINSTON 500
MAY 6, 1984
ALABAMA INTERNATIONAL MOTOR SPEEDWAY
TALLADEGA, ALABAMA
2.66-MILE BANKED TRI-OVAL SUPERSPEEDWAY

Place	Driver	Make	Laps	Money	Pole Pos.
1.	Cale Yarborough	Chev.	188	$42,300	1
2.	Harry Gant	Chev.	188	$31,780	11
3.	Buddy Baker	Ford	188	$22,250	7
4.	Bobby Allison	Buick	188	$31,250	14
5.	Benny Parsons	Chev.	188	$19,650	4
6.	Richard Petty	Pont.	187	$18,495	13
7.	Phil Parsons	Chev.	187	$11,000	21
8.	Dave Marcis	Pont.	187	$16,800	23
9.	Bill Elliott	Ford	187	$14,600	2
10.	Ron Bouchard	Buick	186	$11,525	19

Time of Race: 2 hours, 53 minutes, 27 seconds
Average Speed: 172.988 mph
Margin of Victory: 2 car lengths
Pole Winner: Cale Yarborough, 202.692 mph

"There were a lot of cars that were running pretty well. **You'd catch a draft and you'd be pulled toward the front.** *But as soon as you got there, another line would form and it would go past you."* —CALE YARBOROUGH

1988 Daytona 500

*"To be in front and look in your rearview mirror and see your son, and know that he's **one of the brightest up-and-coming racers** in the sport is a very special feeling."* —BOBBY ALLISON

Davey Allison, the third of the great Allison family drivers, grew up dreaming about racing his father Bobby for victory during the last lap of a major NASCAR Winston Cup Series event.

"In the dreams I always won," said Davey, smiling.

That dream came true—almost—for the twenty-six-year-old Davey on February 14, 1988, in the biggest NASCAR race of all, the Daytona 500. Darrell Waltrip appeared headed to victory after taking the lead six times and holding it for sixty-nine laps. But with fifteen of the two hundred laps remaining, Waltrip's engine soured. This left the Allisons at center stage and a crowd estimated at 135,000 poised to watch a nerve-fraying, father-son show.

With just over a dozen laps to go, Davey hounded Bobby's back bumper until they whipped into the third turn the final time. Davey then pulled to the inside, but couldn't get around and fell in line behind his father.

"I saw Davey coming at me strong the last lap," said a beaming Bobby, then fifty. "I saw the nose of his car out of the corner of my eye. But I was pretty sure my car had too many suds for him.

"What a thrill seeing Davey in my mirror coming through the dog-leg to the checkered flag and knowing we were going to sweep it,"

The Allisons: Daytona's

"Sure I wanted to win. But I had no problems with finishing second to my dad. I've got plenty of Daytona 500s in front of me. I know what this race means to my dad. And **three wins in the Daytona 500 puts the Allison name in an elite circle."** —DAVEY ALLISON

Bobby Allison (12) leads son Davey (28) to the checkered flag in the only 1-2, father-son finish in the history of the Daytona 500.

only father-son, 1-2 finish

B Both Richard Petty, right, and Cale Yarborough, below, left the 1988 Daytona 500 as the result of accidents. Petty's was the more serious of the two but he was not seriously injured. It was Bobby Allison, below right, who coasted to victory in the slowest Daytona since 1960.

said Bobby, after winning the Daytona 500 for the third time and extending his record as the oldest driver to capture a NASCAR Winston Cup Series race. "I tell you, it was great. He did such a wonderful job."

It was only the third 1-2, father-son finish in NASCAR history. Lee and Richard Petty placed 1-2 twice, Lee winning both times.

The victory capped a remarkable Speed Week at Daytona for the elder Allison. He had also won the 125-mile qualifying race leading to the Daytona 500 and the Goody's 300 for NASCAR Busch Series, Grand National Division cars.

"I'm a late bloomer," Bobby stated with a puckish grin.

The Daytona 500 win marked his second straight NASCAR Winston Cup Series triumph on the track, following a Pepsi Firecracker 400 victory in 1987. Allison's eighty-fourth win, which was to prove the last of his career, broke him from a tie for third place on the all-time NASCAR list with Cale Yarborough. Allison now shares the spot with Waltrip.

"I grew up watching Daddy race," said Davey. "I knew he'd make it tough on me, but wouldn't wreck me. I had mixed emotions the last lap. I didn't want to think of it as my dad up there ahead of me until after the checkered flag. I just wanted that car to finish second."

The eyes of both father and son moistened as Bobby responded, "I'm proud to say that Davey is mine."

1988 DAYTONA 500				
FEBRUARY 14, 1988				
DAYTONA INTERNATIONAL SPEEDWAY				
DAYTONA BEACH, FLORIDA				
2.5-MILE BANKED TRI-OVAL SUPERSPEEDWAY				
Place	Driver	Make	Laps	Money	Pole Pos.
1.	Bobby Allison	Buick	200	$202,940	3
2.	Davey Allison	Ford	200	$113,760	2
3.	Phil Parsons	Olds.	200	$81,625	19
4.	Neil Bonnett	Pont.	200	$67,290	14
5.	Terry Labonte	Chev.	200	$62,415	8
6.	Ken Schrader	Chev.	200	$72,215	1
7.	Rusty Wallace	Pont.	200	$59,990	5
8.	Sterling Marlin	Olds.	200	$43,785	12
9.	Buddy Baker	Ford	200	$36,490	16
10.	Dale Earnhardt	Chev.	200	$62,540	6

Time of Race:	3 hours, 36 minutes, 8 seconds
Average Speed:	137.531 mph
Margin of Victory:	2 car lengths
Pole Winner:	Ken Schrader, 198.823 mph

Son Davey Allison drenches his father, below. Opposite: Bobby enjoys some postrace festivities in victory lane. The victory was Bobby's third in the Daytona 500 and the eighty-fourth and last of his career.

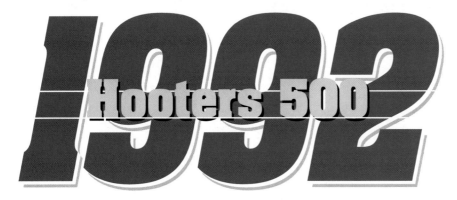

1992 Hooters 500

"When it was over, nobody left. **You had a race winner, a new champion,** *and me running my last race. There was so much going on that everyone just hung around and enjoyed the moment. I wish we had had this much enthusiasm for all the races."*

—RICHARD PETTY

When Alan Kulwicki and Bill Elliott met at the Atlanta Motor Speedway for the Hooters 500, more was at stake than one race. Both drivers were in contention for the NASCAR Winston Cup Series $1 million championship, but were substantially behind points leader Davey Allison, who needed only to finish fifth place or better to secure the prize. The circuit title, based on points accrued throughout the season, was considered an amazing feat for anyone but an impossible dream for a team owner-driver like Kulwicki.

The season finale was noteworthy for two other reasons as well—one whose historical importance was immediately evident, the other only in retrospect. It was the last race for Richard Petty, then fifty-five and the sport's leader with two hundred wins and seven championships. It was also the debut race for a young driver named Jeff Gordon, who would go on to garner multiple championships as well.

The race was not terribly successful for either Gordon or Petty. Petty was swept into a wreck on the 59th of 328 laps. He took his car to the garage for a long period of repairs, then returned so he could be running at the conclusion of his career. Petty finished thirty-fifth. Gordon finished thirty-first after being sidelined by an accident.

Kulwicki wins title as legend's

career ends, another begins

1992 HOOTERS 500
NOVEMBER 15, 1992
ATLANTA MOTOR SPEEDWAY
HAMPTON, GEORGIA
1.522-MILE BANKED OVAL SUPERSPEEDWAY

Place Driver	Make	Laps	Money	Pole Pos.
1. Bill Elliott	Ford	328	$93,800	11
2. Alan Kulwicki	Ford	328	$66,000	14
3. Geoffrey Bodine	Ford	328	$32,400	8
4. Jimmy Spencer	Ford	328	$27,000	18
5. Terry Labonte	Chev.	328	$22,236	6
6. Rusty Wallace	Pont.	328	$20,100	15
7. Sterling Marlin	Ford	327	$18,830	12
8. Jimmy Hensley	Ford	326	$15,900	34
9. Ted Musgrave	Ford	326	$16,600	22
10. Dale Jarrett	Chev.	326	$16,950	32

Time of Race:	3 hours, 44 minutes, 20 seconds
Average Speed:	133.322 mph
Margin of Victory:	7.7 seconds
Pole Winner:	Rick Mast, Oldsmobile, 180.183 mph

The 1992 season finale marked a changing of the guard for NASCAR. It was the final race for fifty-five-year-old Richard Petty, opposite in car 43, whose record two hundred victories almost doubles his closest rival. And it was the first NASCAR race for twenty-one-year-old Jeff Gordon, below.

As the race developed, it was looking like Allison and his team would be a million dollars richer. However, a brush with Ernie Irvan on the 254th lap destroyed Allison's bid for the prize.

"We were just trying to run a smart race," said Allison, sixth when the accident developed. "It looked like Ernie might have had a flat tire and the car got away from him. It's a crusher, but that's the way it goes sometimes. Our team had a great year; we just didn't win the championship."

At the point of Allison's bad luck it appeared that Kulwicki, who had led most of the race, would roll to the title by winning the race. But on the 310th lap Kulwicki pitted for fuel and fell behind Elliott. Now the leader, Elliot came in on 314 and emerged from the pits still ahead.

But Kulwicki had his eye on the big prize. He knew about the five bonus points given to the driver leading the most laps in a race. He also knew that by taking those five points away from Elliott he could avoid the point tie that would award the championship to Elliott based on most victories. Elliott won five times in 1992. Kulwicki had won only twice.

Kulwicki calculated just right. He stayed out long enough to assure that he'd lead 103 laps to Ellott's 102. Hampered by a faulty radio, Elliott's crew was not able to make the laps-led statistic add up in their favor.

"I won, but I lost," said a gracious Elliott. "I'd like to have taken the title for a second time, but to win the last race Richard Petty ever ran is special, so I'll take that. I want to congratulate both Alan and Richard. The effort Alan has put into building his own team is inspiring and terrific."

"It's like I'm living a dream," said Wisconsin native Kulwicki, who appeared stunned by his unexpected success. "This is the answer to a long quest."

Kulwicki was a "privateer" who overcame many problems, most often underfunding, to build his own operation in Charlotte. As both team owner and driver, Kulwicki found himself in the pleasant position of not having to split the $1 million bonus going to the champion.

W

With a 5-2 edge in the tiebreaker win department, all Bill Elliott, left, needed to do to win the NASCAR Winston Cup series title and the $1.3 million champion's share was lead the same number of laps as Alan Kulwicki at Atlanta. He fell one short, 103-102.

1980

World 600

> *"I love [crew chief] David Ifft. But he was so excitable that he was on the radio constantly as I was trying to concentrate on Darrell in those closing laps. He was cheerleading and offering me advice. I got annoyed and distracted. So I told him, 'Please shut up.'"*
>
> —BENNY PARSONS

There they were, side by side—Darrell Waltrip and Benny Parsons—racing toward darkness and, hopefully, the checkered flag.

May 25, 1980, produced one of the strangest scenes and greatest finishes in NASCAR Winston Cup history.

The skies over Charlotte Motor Speedway that spring afternoon were beyond foreboding. They were black. Lightning flashed across the horizon. Twice the skies opened, the downpours forcing delays of forty-seven and forty-eight minutes in NASCAR's longest race.

On the newly paved track matters were just as glum. Four times Harry Gant's right tire blew, the last time taking him out of the race. And on the 267th of 400 laps, points leader Dale Earnhardt blew a tire, lost control, and triggered an accident that eliminated himself, pole-sitter Cale Yarborough, and two other contenders, David Pearson and Bobby Allison.

That left Parsons and Waltrip to battle it out for the victory. They were the last two cars on the lead lap. And they were side by side. With less than forty laps to go, both stopped

for fuel but couldn't risk the time needed to take on fresh rubber.

Seeking to win a record third-straight World 600, Waltrip led after the final exchange of pit stops. But Parsons ran him down and took the lead on the 375th lap. That was the first of six lead swaps between the pair over the last twenty-six laps—five of those coming in the closing twenty miles.

Parsons asked for radio silence from his pits. Waltrip said he had never been more focused. Parsons grabbed the lead on the 399th lap and held on by the margin of a half-car length.

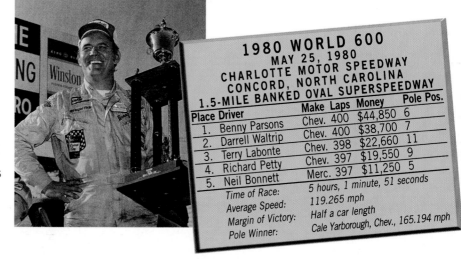

1980 WORLD 600
MAY 25, 1980
CHARLOTTE MOTOR SPEEDWAY
CONCORD, NORTH CAROLINA
1.5-MILE BANKED OVAL SUPERSPEEDWAY

Place	Driver	Make	Laps	Money	Pole Pos.
1.	Benny Parsons	Chev.	400	$44,850	6
2.	Darrell Waltrip	Chev.	400	$38,700	7
3.	Terry Labonte	Chev.	398	$22,660	11
4.	Richard Petty	Chev.	397	$19,550	9
5.	Neil Bonnett	Merc.	397	$11,250	5

Time of Race: 5 hours, 1 minute, 51 seconds
Average Speed: 119.265 mph
Margin of Victory: Half a car length
Pole Winner: Cale Yarborough, Chev., 165.194 mph

Waltrip, Parsons swap

"I don't know if two cars ever raced that long together side by side."

—DARRELL WALTRIP

The Chevrolet Monte Carlos of race winner Benny Parsons (27) and Darrell Waltrip lead Neil Bonnett's Mercury (21) out of a turn at Charlotte Motor Speedway late in the race.

Parsons, opposite, recalls the 1980 World 600 as "the best driver-against-driver battle I'd ever been in."

leads five times in final minutes

1999 Daytona 500

"Beating Earnhardt like that in the Daytona 500 is probably the biggest single thrill I've had."

—JEFF GORDON

NASCAR's two biggest stars, Jeff Gordon and Dale Earnhardt, met in a duel of strategy and reflexes in the 1999 Daytona 500. Gordon masterfully blocked the best moves of Earnhardt over an exciting final ten laps and won a battle of the Rainbow Warrior and the Intimidator.

Gordon hurtled around the 33-degree banking of the 2.5-mile track with Earnhardt only inches behind. Earnhardt was right on Gordon's rear bumper the last pulsating twenty-five miles, feinting both inside and out in a futile effort to find a way around.

"He was setting me up every lap, and I really thought he was going to get me. . . . It is a dream come true for me to race Dale Earnhardt all the way to the line in the Daytona 500," said Gordon, who won by a car length. "It doesn't get any better than this. I want to thank Dale for a great race. And I also want to thank him for what he's taught me the past couple years. That's the only way I kept him behind me."

Said Earnhardt, after coming close to scoring a second straight victory in the

Place	Driver	Make	Laps	Money	Pole Pos.
1.	Jeff Gordon	Chev.	200	$2,172,246	1
2.	Dale Earnhardt	Chev.	200	$613,659	4
3.	Kenny Irwin	Ford	200	$440,584	41
4.	Mike Skinner	Chev.	200	$350,634	12
5.	Michael Waltrip	Chev.	200	$290,596	13
6.	Ken Schrader	Chev.	200	$186,731	7
7.	Kyle Petty	Pont.	200	$145,809	24
8.	Rusty Wallace	Ford	200	$173,209	10
9.	Chad Little	Ford	200	$142,884	26
10.	Rick Mast	Ford	200	$139,096	21

1999 DAYTONA 500
FEBRUARY 14, 1999
DAYTONA INTERNATIONAL SPEEDWAY
DAYTONA BEACH, FLORIDA
2.5-MILE BANKED TRI-OVAL SUPERSPEEDWAY

Time of Race: 3 hours, 5 minutes, 42 seconds
Average Speed: 161.551 mph
Margin of Victory: .128 second
Pole Winner: Jeff Gordon, 195.067 mph

Student Gordon

Jeff Gordon celebrates after his Daytona 500 win over Dale Earnhardt. The Daytona win was Gordon's 43rd career victory out of 190 starts. No driver in NASCAR history has garnered that many wins faster.

edges out master Earnhardt

NASCAR Winston Cup Series classic that previously had eluded him for twenty years, "If I could have just gotten to him in the corners, I might have gotten under him and won. But I couldn't get there. I got beat. Anyone who could survive that last ten laps, it was awesome just to come home and finish."

After the checkered flag, Earnhardt pulled alongside his younger rival and swerved slightly into Gordon's car. Earnhardt gave a wave of congratulations. "He was showing me how much fun he'd had," said Gordon, winner of the 500 for the second time in three years.

"I wanted it bad and he wanted it bad. That's why it was such a great race."

Dale Earnhardt (3) pounds on the rear bumper of Jeff Gordon (24) as the leaders move under Mike Skinner (31) late in the 1999 Daytona 500.

Above: A NASCAR official holds Jeff Gordon at the end of pit row for a fifteen-second penalty early in the race. Gordon was penalized for having too many crew members over the wall during an earlier pit stop.

During a caution period the Valvoline crew performs a four-tire stop on Mark Martin's Ford, rushing to beat Jeff Gordon out of the pits. Martin finished toward the end of the pack due to handling problems.

"That was as good a race as I've ever seen. There were so many things going on. Was Earnhardt going to get Gordon? Was Mike Skinner going to help Dale out and double-team Jeff? Gordon didn't have a bit of help and held Dale off. That was a great victory."

—TERRY LABONTE, GORDON'S TEAMMATE

"Give Gordon credit.
He beat me."

—DALE EARNHARDT

Having battled off one last challenge by Dale Earnhardt (3), Jeff Gordon (24) dives to the checkered flag. The final ten laps of the 1999 Daytona 500 provided the capacity crowd with a thrilling duel between NASCAR's two most popular drivers. Following the leaders to the finish were third-place Kenny Irwin (in the Texaco Havoline Ford) and Earnhardt's teammate Mike Skinner (in the Lowe's Chevrolet). Gordon's win gave the young driver his second Daytona 500 victory while preventing a repeat by the Intimidator, who had finally garnered his first Daytona 500 win the year before.

Incredible

Comebacks

The races in which drivers were down but not out—and came back to win

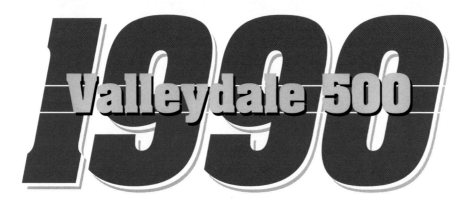

1990 Valleydale 500

"We both played it by the book. I held my line. I didn't mirror drive. I gave him some room to race and he didn't come up into me.

We were going to make each other earn it fair and square.

You can't make it cleaner or closer."

—Davey Allison

Things didn't look so hot for Davey Allison early in the 1990 Valleydale 500 at Bristol International Raceway. Allison had been mired deep in the field much of the race, falling back after an early accident. If he was going to have a shot at even placing in this race, he and his team would need to take a few risks.

Allison's team owner, Robert Yates, explained the pivotal strategy. "We had the car dialed in, handling well, and we only had thirty-three laps on the tires at the time. We needed to get up front. There were ten other cars on the lead lap and we couldn't afford to be behind all of them. So we gambled on seeing what would happen if we didn't pit."

Allison regained track position on the 391st of the 500 laps, forgoing a pit stop while the other leaders pitted. He led the final 109 laps, brilliantly battling Darrell Waltrip and then Mark Martin.

The finish was so close as Allison and Martin sped side by side under the checkered flag that NASCAR officials delayed declaring a winner in order to view a videotape of the action. It was determined that Allison finished ahead of Martin by less than six inches.

"Unbelievable!" said Allison, who won at the bowl-shaped track for the first time. "I concentrated on running my line and making

Davey Allison forgoes pits to

Darrell Waltrip (17) hugged Davey Allison's rear bumper for forty straight laps before a flat tire ended Waltrip's challenge with twenty-five laps to go and turned over second place to Mark Martin.

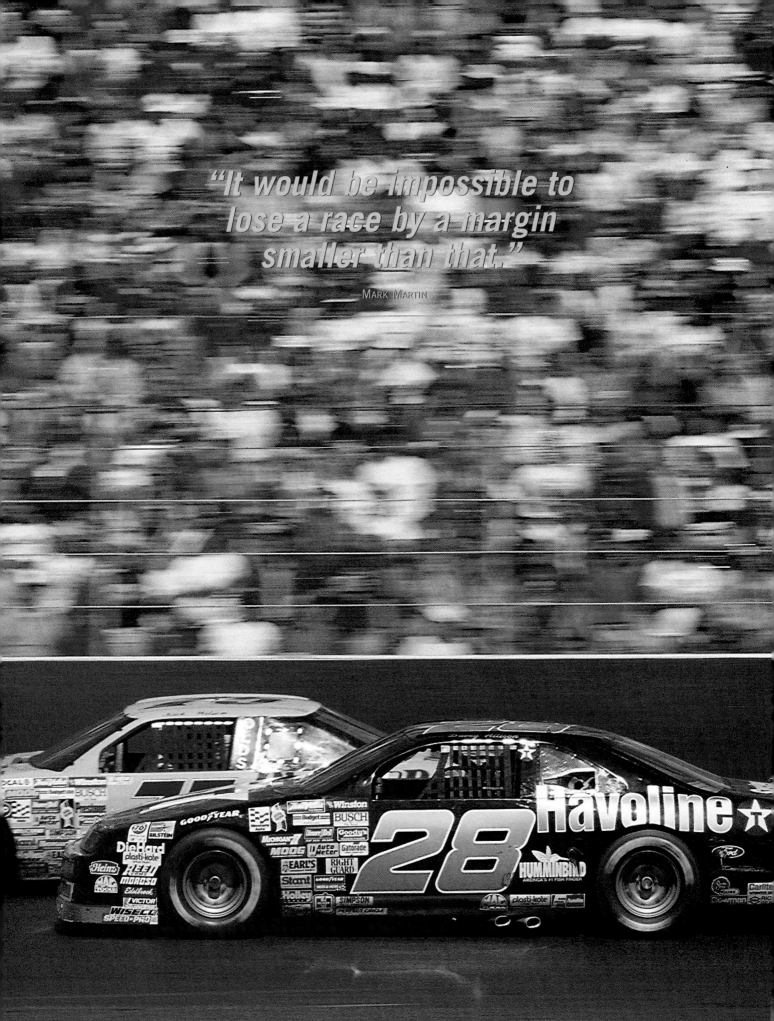

"It would be impossible to lose a race by a margin smaller than that."

—MARK MARTIN

Mark earn it if he won. He got a good run going at me from the inside off turn four and almost beat me."

"Boy, it was close," said Martin. "I did all I could, but there just wasn't enough racetrack to get by Davey. I gave it a last shot, figuring that even if I crashed I would make it across the line in second place."

The race produced uncommon contact, leading seventeen of the thirty-two starters to either touch or spin. Out of that contact developed a comical incident as the race concluded.

Ricky Rudd and Sterling Marlin were battling for third place when they bumped on the last lap. Marlin spun as a result. After both took the checkered flag, Marlin stopped and waited on Rudd in turn three. When Rudd saw the revenge-minded Marlin, he stopped, too. Marlin began backing up, and so did Rudd in a humorous chase in reverse toward turn two. Finally, Marlin motored forward to pit row and Rudd followed.

"I didn't want to see Sterling wreck," said Rudd. "It was just hard racing."

Davey Allison spent much of the Valleydale 500 battling traffic deep in the pack after an early tussle with Rob Moroso. Opposite, Allison's Ford (28) ducks to the inside of Rick Wilson's Pontiac.

Late in the race, Ricky Rudd (5) passed Sterling Marlin (94) to finish third, above. Chasing is the lapped car of Ernie Irvan.

1990 VALLEYDALE 500
APRIL 8, 1990
BRISTOL INTERNATIONAL RACEWAY
BRISTOL, TENNESSEE
.533-MILE PAVED OVAL

Place	Driver	Make	Laps	Money	Pole Pos.
1.	Davey Allison	Ford	500	$50,100	19
2.	Mark Martin	Ford	500	$31,300	3
3.	Ricky Rudd	Chev.	500	$19,775	13
4.	Terry Labonte	Olds.	500	$13,500	14
5.	Rick Wilson	Pont.	500	$13,857	25
6.	Ken Schrader	Chev.	500	$11,675	17
7.	Sterling Marlin	Olds.	500	$9,850	5
8.	Morgan Shepherd	Ford	499	$8,475	15
9.	Darrell Waltrip	Chev.	499	$25,500	19
10.	Kyle Petty	Pont.	499	$11,900	4

Time of Race:	3 hours, 3 minutes, 16 seconds
Average Speed:	187.258 mph
Margin of Victory:	6 inches
Pole Winner:	Ernie Irvan, Olds., 116.157 mph

1963 Daytona 500

"I wanted to win for Marvin and for the Wood Brothers because they took a chance."

—TINY LUND

DeWayne "Tiny" Lund was a down-and-out racer when he departed the South Carolina fishing camp he operated early in February 1963, bound for the Daytona 500.

He had eighteen cents in his pocket and no significant hopes of driving in the race. His main goals were to meet some friends and, hopefully, make contact with a car owner in search of a driver.

When he returned home later that month, Lund was both a hero and a champion—the star of one of the warmest chapters in the history of NASCAR.

On February 14, Lund was standing with a group of five individuals when the Maserati that Marvin Panch was testing for the 24 Hours of Daytona sports car race flipped and caught fire with the helpless driver trapped inside.

Lund rushed to the scene with his four friends and, using the strength in his 6-foot-6, 275-pound body, helped pull Panch from the flaming wreckage.

Hospitalized with burns so severe that he had to withdraw from the Daytona 500, Panch asked his car owners, the famed Glen and Leonard Wood, to hire Lund as his substitute. The Wood Brothers agreed.

Fast forward to the fairytale ending.

Tiny Lund won the Daytona 500 in a finish that was almost as implausible as the events leading up to the race.

The Wood Brothers never changed tires on Lund's car. They stretched out the gas mileage and made one less pit stop than the other contenders. And Lund took the checkered flag on his first top-echelon NASCAR victory as his Ford ran out of gas.

1963 DAYTONA 500
FEBRUARY 24, 1963
DAYTONA INTERNATIONAL SPEEDWAY
DAYTONA BEACH, FLORIDA
2.5-MILE BANKED TRI-OVAL SUPERSPEEDWAY

Place	Driver	Make	Laps	Money	Pole Pos.
1.	Tiny Lund	Ford	200	$24,550	12
2.	Fred Lorenzen	Ford	200	$15,450	2
3.	Ned Jarrett	Ford	200	$8,700	6
4.	Nelson Stacy	Ford	199	$6,275	10
5.	Dan Gurney	Ford	199	$3,550	11

Time of Race: 3 hours, 17 minutes, 56 seconds
Average Speed: 151.566 mph
Margin of Victory: 24 seconds
Pole Winner: Fireball Roberts, Pont., 160.943 mph

Lund earns winning

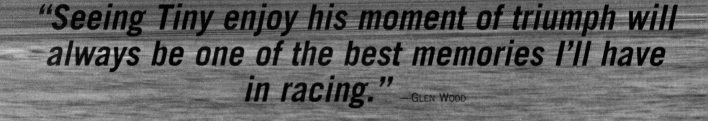

"Seeing Tiny enjoy his moment of triumph will always be one of the best memories I'll have in racing." —GLEN WOOD

Given the injured Panch's ride in the Daytona 500, Lund, above, chases the pole-sitting Pontiac of Fireball Roberts (22). He won the Daytona 500 in one of the biggest Cinderella stories in motorsports history. Right: After the race, Lund received his awards in near disbelief.

ride by rescuing Panch

1984
Talladega 500

"One second I had the lead, and the next second I'm in the middle of this pack with cars all around me. A lot of fans said that was **the most exciting finish ever.** *I know my heart skipped a beat or two."* —TERRY LABONTE

Driver Dale Earnhardt was fuming all week before the Talladega 500. He felt his driving style had been impugned when early in the week some drivers charged that the usually aggressive Earnhardt had become a "stroker," or gone conservative. This was cited as the reason for Earnhardt leading the point standings toward the NASCAR Winston Cup Series championship despite his lack of a win.

The criticism had Earnhardt seething.

"Just because I hadn't won this year they were taking shots at me," said Earnhardt. "I had finished second four times, right on the bumpers of the winners almost, and I was supposed to be stroking. Now that doesn't make sense."

If ever there was a race in which blatant nonassertiveness would have been evident, this was the one. There were a whopping sixty-eight lead changes among sixteen drivers. As the race approached its final lap, ten drivers battled in the tightly bunched, lead aerodynamic draft. Any of the ten conceivably could have won.

Terry Labonte held a tenuous lead over the other nine drivers. But on turn four of the 2.66-mile track, Earnhardt swung outside for a pass. Earnhardt's unusual outside route to make the pivotal pass of Labonte was certainly not the easiest way to get around.

Earnhardt fends off critics

Dale Earnhardt celebrates his tenth career NASCAR Winston Cup victory—and his first for car owner Richard Childress—in the 1984 Talladega 500.

with last-lap charge

"You go into every race wanting to win. But **I really wanted to win** that race. I hadn't won yet in 1984 and I heard what people were saying. I needed an answer."

—DALE EARNHARDT

Dale Earnhardt (3) pulls the draft into a turn of the 1984 Talladega 500. Tucked in behind Earnhardt's Chevrolet are Geoffrey Bodine, Cale Yarborough, Richard Petty, Bobby Allison, and Terry Labonte.

"Terry favored the inside the last few laps," said Earnhardt. "So the last time around I held my car straight in the higher line coming off turn two and went on. I went outside because I figured it was too muddy to race in the infield."

The pack of other drivers went abreast in Earnhardt's wake and began dicing for position. But Earnhardt held on, even widening his lead to a 1.66-second margin of victory—the biggest advantage any driver held under the green flag. As the drivers crossed the finish line, Labonte appeared to salvage second place in a photo finish with Buddy Baker, Bobby Allison, and Cale Yarborough. However, two hours after the checkered flag and careful study of pictures from three cameras by NASCAR officials, Baker was placed second and Labonte third.

Quick pit stops by the Richard Childress crew helped keep Earnhardt near the lead throughout the long afternoon.

"This undoubtedly is the most exciting race I've ever been involved in," said Earnhardt. "There always seemed to be ten or twelve of us up there fighting for the lead. Every little bit you'd find yourself racing different guys for position."

Earnhardt, becoming the first back-to-back winner of Talladega 500s, averaged 155.485 mph in scoring the tenth triumph of his career.

"As I came through turn four my car owner, Richard Childress, and others on the team were yelling over the radio, 'Drive that thing! Drive that thing!' I started to answer with something cute, but about that time I saw Buddy and Terry side by side in my mirror, and I pretty well knew the race was mine. So I drove with my right hand and waved to the crew and the fans with my left all the way through the homestretch.

"Just call me 'Stroker,'" Earnhardt said with an impish grin.

1984 TALLADEGA 500
JULY 29, 1984
ALABAMA INTERNATIONAL MOTOR SPEEDWAY
TALLADEGA, ALABAMA
2.66-MILE BANKED TRI-OVAL SUPERSPEEDWAY

Place	Driver	Make	Laps	Money	Pole Pos.
1.	Dale Earnhardt	Chev.	188	$47,100	3
2.	Buddy Baker	Ford	188	$28,225	6
3.	Terry Labonte	Chev.	188	$22,455	4
4.	Bobby Allison	Buick	188	$24,350	16
5.	Cale Yarborough	Chev.	188	$15,350	1
6.	Darrell Waltrip	Chev.	188	$17,200	7
7.	Harry Gant	Chev.	188	$11,395	14
8.	Lake Speed	Chev.	188	$6,050	15
9.	Tommy Ellis	Chev.	188	$5,950	5
10.	Bill Elliott	Ford	188	$12,750	2

Time of Race: 3 hours, 12 minutes, 4 seconds
Average Speed: 155.485 mph
Margin of Victory: 1.66 seconds
Pole Winner: Cale Yarborough, 202.474 mph

1985
Winston 500

"I honestly didn't think we could make the two laps up. I needed a caution. But I didn't get any until very late in the race. [Our winning] was a credit to the crew." —BILL ELLIOTT

The 1985 Winston 500 was going to be an important race for Bill Elliott. Tobacco giant R. J. Reynolds had put up a new $1 million prize and Elliott was in the running for it. Elliott led twenty-five laps in the early going, battling Kyle Petty, Cale Yarborough, and Dale Earnhardt for first place. But on the 48th of the 188-lap race at Alabama International Motor Speedway, an oil scavenger line worked loose in a puff of smoke. Elliott had to pit for repairs.

"I almost panicked when my crew had to raise the hood to fix that oil line," said the redheaded Elliott, who had qualified at a NASCAR record 209.398 mph. "I thought it was all over for us."

When Elliott got back on the track he was almost five miles—close to two laps—behind leader Yarborough. But by turning laps at a sizzling 205 mph, Elliott unlapped himself on lap 125 and whipped back into the lead on lap 145. He made up his deficit in a green-flag charge, overtaking and passing Yarborough without the benefit of a distance-erasing yellow flag.

Once Elliott regained first place, there was little doubt about the outcome.

Elliott bridges whopping

Third-place Cale Yarborough (left) joins winner Bill Elliott during the victory celebration following the 1985 Winston 500 at Talladega.

Opposite: After rallying from almost two laps down, Bill Elliott's Ford Thunderbird (9) passes Cale Yarborough to reclaim the lead on the 145th of 188 trips around NASCAR's largest tri-oval superspeedway.

five-mile gap to pass Yarborough

"Bill was in another area code," joked Petty, who edged Yarborough in a photo finish for second place, 1.72 seconds behind Elliott.

"I'm happy with the way I ran," said Yarborough. "But I couldn't do anything with Elliott. No one could. Bill had the gas pedal on the floor the whole race, and his car was handling so well he could drive it anywhere he wanted. That's an unbeatable combination."

The victory put Elliott two-thirds of the way toward a $1 million bonus posted that season for the first time by R. J. Reynolds Tobacco Company. The prize rewards a driver who scores at least three victories in the Big Four of NASCAR racing.

Elliott, who won the Daytona 500 in February, failed to take the Winston Million in Charlotte's World 600 but got another shot in the Southern 500 at Darlington, South Carolina, later in the season.

The Talladega triumph was Elliott's fourth in five superspeedway races so far that season, tying him with his boyhood hero, David Pearson, for the best start ever. And that success earned Elliott a new nickname: "Awesome Bill From Dawsonville."

At the time, Elliott seemed embarrassed by the acclaim.

"I don't consider myself a star," he said. "I mean, I'm not on a pedestal or anything like that. I'm not that type of person."

The raising of the hood in a NASCAR Winston Cup Series race usually signals defeat. But Bill Elliott's crew repaired a broken oil line before his rivals could twice circle the 2.66-mile oval at Talladega, Alabama, opposite. Then Elliott made up the deficit without the aid of a caution and scored one of the greatest comeback victories in racing history.

Bill Elliott's victory at Talladega set the stage for his triumph in the Winston Million. His win in the Winston 500 followed an almost equally impressive victory in the Daytona 500.

"How impressive was Elliott? . . . The guys in my crew would tell me,

'Elliott is really flying.'"

—KYLE PETTY

1985 WINSTON 500
MAY 5, 1985
ALABAMA INTERNATIONAL MOTOR SPEEDWAY
TALLADEGA, ALABAMA
2.66-MILE BANK TRI-OVAL SUPERSPEEDWAY

Place	Driver	Make	Laps	Money	Pole Pos.
1.	Bill Elliott	Ford	188	$60,500	1
2.	Kyle Petty	Ford	188	$34,905	4
3.	Cale Yarborough	Ford	188	$37,750	2
4.	Bobby Allison	Buick	187	$23,075	17
5.	Ricky Rudd	Ford	187	$21,025	15
6.	Buddy Baker	Olds.	185	$20,245	32
7.	Terry Labonte	Chev.	185	$20,100	3
8.	Dave Marcis	Chev.	185	$12,575	18
9.	Bobby Hillin Jr.	Chev.	184	$7,800	7
10.	Lake Speed	Pont.	183	$11,215	20

Time of Race:	2 hours, 41 minutes, 4 seconds
Average Speed:	186.288 mph
Margin of Victory:	1.72 seconds
Pole Winner:	Bill Elliott, 209.938 mph

1998
Napa 500

"Everyone in the garages applauds what Rudd did today and what he has done over sixteen straight years. **To me, that's one of the great streaks in sports."** —ERNIE IRVAN

Even under normal conditions the tight, flat .526-mile Martinsville Speedway, shaped somewhat like a paper clip, takes a toll on the machines and the men driving them. It was especially tough at the 1998 Napa 500: The air temperature was near 95 degrees and far higher in the cars. So it had to be a very determined Ricky Rudd who overcame driver-wilting heat and superstars Jeff Gordon and Mark Martin in the Napa 500 to extend a remarkable NASCAR winning streak.

When the cooling system malfunctioned in Rudd's Ford, the driver endured excruciating conditions beyond any experienced by his foes. "I was sweltering in there," said Rudd, who stretched out on the pavement of victory lane to receive treatment with oxygen and fluids after taking the checkered flag. "I really had to work on myself mentally. . . . If there's such a thing as blocking out pain, I did it."

Rudd suffered blisters on his back and buttocks because the seat in his car got so hot. "It was

Determined Rudd braves heat,

"I was listening to him on my scanner when he said the fan was not working. I admire him for his **courage to stay in that car** and to go on—and win the race."

—NASCAR FAN BRIAN WEAVER, MARTINSVILLE, VIRGINIA

Ricky Rudd wrestles with the air hose to his helmet during a pit stop in an unsuccessful attempt to fix the failed driver cooling system in his Ford, opposite. Although the heat in the cockpit was oppressive to the point of raising medical concerns, Rudd led 198 of the 500 laps, including the final 96 to the checkered flag.

blisters to take flag

"I was caught in the middle. The car was so good that I couldn't afford to get out because **I knew we could win.** But I didn't know if my body was going to hold up to the finish." —RICKY RUDD

like sitting on an iron, knowing you're getting burned, but ignoring the pain for three and a half hours."

Rudd knew early on what he faced. The system used to cool both his body and the seat had failed. By the twenty-fifth lap he was radioing his crew to find a relief driver. Veteran Hut Stricklin was summoned to the pit to stand by. "I thought about getting out, but my car was so darn good I couldn't make myself do it," said Rudd. "I could taste victory lane."

Rudd took the lead with ninety-six laps to go and held on against his own fading strength and the challenges of Gordon and Martin the rest of the way. Gordon was the runner-up, .533 seconds behind.

Chris Pinto, a crewman for Rudd, looked at the wan driver smiling weakly in triumph.

Praised Pinto, "One thing didn't overheat, and that's Ricky's heart."

Although near exhaustion and suffering from heat-related illness, Rudd was able to receive medical treatment, below, then pose seated with the Napa 500 trophy next to the hood of his Ford, opposite, after extending his streak to scoring at least one win in sixteen straight seasons.

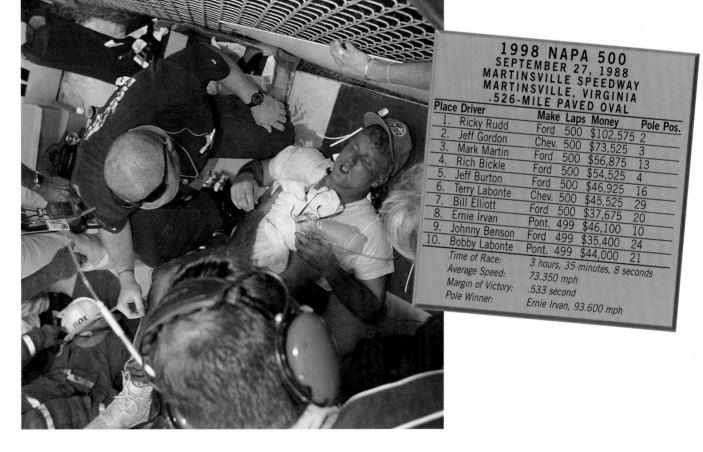

1998 NAPA 500
SEPTEMBER 27, 1988
MARTINSVILLE SPEEDWAY
MARTINSVILLE, VIRGINIA
.526-MILE PAVED OVAL

Place	Driver	Make	Laps	Money	Pole Pos.
1.	Ricky Rudd	Ford	500	$102,575	2
2.	Jeff Gordon	Chev.	500	$73,525	3
3.	Mark Martin	Ford	500	$56,875	13
4.	Rich Bickle	Ford	500	$54,525	4
5.	Jeff Burton	Ford	500	$46,925	16
6.	Terry Labonte	Chev.	500	$45,525	29
7.	Bill Elliott	Ford	500	$37,675	20
8.	Ernie Irvan	Pont.	499	$46,100	10
9.	Johnny Benson	Ford	499	$35,400	24
10.	Bobby Labonte	Pont.	499	$44,000	21

Time of Race: 3 hours, 35 minutes, 8 seconds
Average Speed: 73.350 mph
Margin of Victory: .533 second
Pole Winner: Ernie Irvan, 93.600 mph

*"When I learned that Ricky drove in those conditions without any cooling, it made his victory **all that more impressive.**"* —JEFF BURTON

1988
Oakwood Homes 500

"*For me,* **that was my most hair raising race**—*[to be] three miles down and win right at the end. I was sweating like crazy when I got out of the car because there's controversy. Everyone's saying there's no way a car can be fast enough to make up three miles.*"

—RUSTY WALLACE

I"It's the biggest win of my career," said an excited Rusty Wallace as he exulted in victory lane after the 1988 Oakwood Homes 500. "I didn't know if I could get back into contention or not, and then I didn't know if I could hold Darrell off or not."

Fairly early in the race at Charlotte Motor Speedway, a sputtering engine put Wallace three miles behind. On lap 112, Wallace pitted for work on the ignition, which was suspected as the source of the trouble. By lap 139 the engine was still missing so Wallace returned to the pit for a change of carburetors, losing one lap. That fixed the problem for the time being but a discovery that the air cleaner had been left off during the previous stop put Wallace back in the pit on lap 142, costing him a second lap.

Wallace regained one lap during a restart on lap 222 after a very timely

Timely cautions let Wallace

NASCAR 25 GREATEST RACES

Rusty Wallace's tenacious rally from two laps down in the second race at Charlotte Motor Speedway in 1988 helped the thirty-two-year-old driver finish second in the final NASCAR Winston Cup standings. Wallace won the title with car owner Raymond Beadle the following season.

"This has to be one of the greatest races ever. The determination and hard work *that it took Wallace to come back was unbelievable!"* —NASCAR FAN BRANDON LEWIS, MIDDLESBORO, KENTUCKY

KODIAK

GOOD/YEAR

76

BILSTEIN

ieHard
CRANE Cams
Stewart
MOROSO

Tru Value · Winston · NASCAR
TRW · BUSCH · Goody's
MICHIGAN · MOOG
STEWART WARNER · PEAK · Gatorade
SPEED PRO · Holley
EARL'S
SIMPSON

Rusty Wallace

27

make up three miles for win

"I thought I won. I was asking all the officials, 'Show me the scoring charts, prove it.' They showed me. But part of me still says there was a mistake and that I won. **I'm stubborn like that."**

—DARRELL WALTRIP

caution period. He got the other back in a restart on lap 285 after another providential caution, joining Waltrip and five others for torrid, close-quarters racing the rest of the way.

Then Wallace's engine began to skip again. Although his car was running on just 7½ cylinders, Wallace snagged the lead twelve laps from the finish and somehow managed to stay there the rest of the way.

"I've never been part of anything like this," gushed Wallace.

During the 334th and final lap Waltrip maneuvered high in the banking of the first and second turns, trying to pass Wallace on the outside. This didn't work, so Waltrip ducked inside at the end of the backstretch and almost pulled abreast of Wallace going into turn three. Wallace forced Waltrip to the flat apron and the latter had to back off the throttle. Wallace similarly foiled Waltrip's inside move off turn four.

"That's the widest Pontiac I ever followed," Waltrip said of Wallace's car, fielded by the Blue Max team. "It could have been real bad there at the end if I'd wanted it to be and forced the issue. But I drove the right kind of race—clean."

The two were so close down the back straight it appeared that Waltrip actually pushed Wallace part of the way.

Waltrip congratulated Wallace, but then questioned whether a scoring mixup might have credited Wallace with making up too much of his deficit. "I think he was on the tail end of the lead lap," said Waltrip.

NASCAR rechecked, then ruled otherwise.

After winning the Coca-Cola 600 over the Memorial Day weekend, Darrell Waltrip, below and opposite, thought he was headed for a sweep of the 1988 races at Charlotte Motor Speedway. That was before Rusty Wallace's rally.

1988 OAKWOOD HOMES 500				
OCTOBER 9, 1988				
CHARLOTTE MOTOR SPEEDWAY				
CONCORD, NORTH CAROLINA				
1.5-MILE BANKED TRI-OVAL SUPERSPEEDWAY				
Place Driver	Make	Laps	Money	Pole Pos.
1. Rusty Wallace	Pont.	334	$84,300	3
2. Darrell Waltrip	Chev.	334	$54,525	10
3. Brett Bodine	Ford	334	$43,350	18
4. Bill Elliott	Ford	334	$35,900	2
5. Sterling Marlin	Olds.	334	$28,200	9
6. Bobby Hillin Jr.	Buick	334	$20,740	32
7. Ken Schrader	Chev.	334	$16,300	7
8. Ricky Rudd	Buick	334	$13,625	36
9. Mark Martin	Ford	334	$13,850	4
10. Terry Labonte	Chev.	334	$15,350	24
Time of Race:	3 hours, 50 minutes, 2 seconds			
Average Speed:	130.677 mph			
Margin of Victory:	1 car length			
Pole Winner:	Alan Kulwicki, Ford, 176.896 mph			

Fabulous

Finishes

The races that were made memorable in their final seconds

1976
Daytona 500

*"Whenever David and I hooked up, everyone knew it was going to be exciting. **We raced hard.**"*

—RICHARD PETTY

After 499¾ miles of full-bore racing on asphalt, the Daytona 500 was decided on grass at a speed of about 20 mph. What loomed as a classic confrontation all the way to the checkered flag between NASCAR's two biggest stars, Richard Petty and David Pearson, instead evolved into a grinding final lap incident.

Petty, seeking a sixth triumph in the 500, led as he and Pearson took the white flag signaling the last of the race's two hundred laps. Pearson, going for a first win in the sport's biggest event, passed Petty for the lead at the end of the backstretch. Petty immediately dived inside in turn three and the two touched sheet metal. Petty was almost past Pearson as they sped off turn four toward the tri-oval homestretch when there was harder contact. Both drivers now careened out of control, their cars sustaining significant damage.

Petty wound up stalled approximately one hundred feet short of the flag stand. As Petty frantically tried to get his Dodge refired, Pearson somehow got his Mercury moving again and angled across the turf to take the flag.

"I asked the Wood Brothers on the radio where Richard was . . . if he had spun across the finish line," said Pearson.

The crumpled front end of Pearson's Mercury made for a capable trophy stand.

Pearson crawls to finish

after famed brush with Petty

David Pearson, the shrewd Silver Fox of stock car racing, leads before tucking his Mercury in behind Richard Petty for slingshot pass position.

"When they told me no, I took off as hard as I could, which wasn't very hard at all. It seemed like I was a mile from the line and that it took forever to get there. . . . Even so, I'm tickled to win. If we had backed across to win, it would have been okay."

Pearson had the presence of mind during the accident to push in his clutch and keep the car's engine running. As the incident unfolded, a member of Pearson's Wood Brothers team instinctively yelled a warning via radio, "There's a wreck off turn four!"

And Pearson coolly replied, "Yeah, I know. I'm in it." Pearson had spun out while leading the Daytona 500 with only three laps to go in 1975, winding up in fourth place. From that day on he'd made winning the race his greatest goal.

Petty generally accepted blame for the stunning, decisive incident on the last lap. "I wasn't all the way by David when we hit," said Petty. "I hadn't cleared him."

Some of Petty's crewmen dashed across pit row to give their car a push and get it going again. Their effort was to no avail.

NASCAR penalized Petty a lap for the crew's action, which was against the rules, but he finished second nonetheless.

"I had one ulcer before the race," joked Petty, flashing his famous smile. "Now I've got two."

As 125,000 spectators and NASCAR's first live national television audience watched, Pearson passed Petty as planned on the backstretch of the last lap. But Pearson drifted high in turn three. Petty dove to the inside when both cars broke loose from the track in the fourth turn and slammed into the outside wall.

Petty slid into the infield with a dead engine. Pearson managed to engage the clutch and keep his car running.

Pearson's car slowly began to creep forward, moving past Petty's crumpled hulk and back onto the track where it rolled to the checkered flag.

"Man, what a finish!
Now *that* is what never giving up is all about."

—NASCAR FAN JERRY W. RAY, ALABASTER, ALABAMA

1976 DAYTONA 500
FEBRUARY 15, 1976
DAYTONA BEACH, FLORIDA
DAYTONA INTERNATIONAL SPEEDWAY
2.5-MILE BANKED TRI-OVAL SUPERSPEEDWAY

Place	Driver	Make	Laps	Money	Pole Pos.
1.	David Pearson	Merc.	200	$48,800	7
2.	Richard Petty	Dodge	199	$35,750	6
3.	Benny Parsons	Chev.	199	$23,680	32
4.	Lennie Pond	Chev.	198	$15,890	11
5.	Neil Bonnett	Chev.	197	$14,000	13
6.	Terry Ryan	Chev.	196	$13,800	2
7.	J. D. McDuffie	Chev.	193	$11,260	41
8.	Terry Bivins	Chev.	193	$9,685	19
9.	Richard Childress	Chev.	191	$8,990	36
10.	Frank Warren	Dodge	190	$8,340	34

Time of Race:	3 hours, 17 minutes, 8 seconds
Average Speed:	152.181 mph
Margin of Victory:	60 yards
Pole Winner:	Ramo Stott, Chev., 183.450 mph

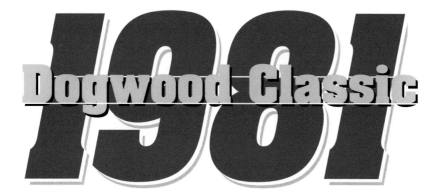

1981 Dogwood Classic

"My crew was yelling on the radio, 'There's a big crash at the finish,' and I thought I might win. But when I got there, both Richie and Geoffrey had managed to get their wrecks across the line.

How, I don't know."

—JERRY COOK

H. Clay Earles, the founder of Martinsville Speedway, minced no words when it came to describing the finish of the 1981 Dogwood Classic for NASCAR's Modified Division.

"Greatest finish I ever saw," Earles said years later.

"We've had bigger races and faster races and better races from start to finish. But at the checkered flag, I'd never seen one like that before or since."

It's safe to say Earles was right, since seldom do cars approach the finish line driving perpendicular to the track on the outside wall as Richie Evans did.

Evans had tangled with Geoffrey Bodine coming off the fourth turn of the 250th and final lap. The impact destroyed Bodine's front suspension and left his car crippled in the middle of the

track. Evans' car, meantime, was catapulted into the outside wall—the underbody pinned to the concrete and catch fence as the rear wheels were still spinning.

"Richie never got off the gas," said Earles. "You could read the roof number from the infield. He rode the wall until just before the finish when the car bounced onto the track and crossed the finish line on three wheels."

1981 DOGWOOD CLASSIC
MARCH 15, 1981
MARTINSVILLE SPEEDWAY
MARTINSVILLE, VIRGINIA
.526-MILE PAVED OVAL

Place	Driver	Make	Laps	Money	Pole Pos.
1.	Richie Evans	Pinto	250	$9,250	5
2.	Geoffrey Bodine	Pinto	250	$5,725	1
3.	John Blewett Jr.	Grem.	250	$2,850	11
4.	Jerry Cook	Pinto	250	$1,400	10
5.	Maynard Troyer	Pinto	250	$1,300	4

Time of Race: 2 hours, 4 minutes, 24 seconds
Average Speed: 63.370 mph
Margin of Victory: 3.5 seconds
Pole Winner: Geoffrey Bodine, 96.693 mph

Evans takes Modified

With the remnants of his modified as background, Richie Evans accepts the Dogwood Classic trophy, opposite, after the wild finish. Evans had bounced onto the front straight wall after a collision with Geoffrey Bodine, above, and rode the wall sideways, hitting the pavement with his three remaining tires just before the finish line, right.

flag on three wheels

1987 The Winston

> "That was the one pass that I have already told my kids about and **will probably tell my grandchildren about.**"
>
> —NASCAR FAN RON SHUE, FREMONT, OHIO

With only ten laps left, everyone thought the Winston All-Star Race would be an anticlimactic race for the third straight year. Driver Bill Elliott had led 121 of the first 125 laps, and at one point he was ahead by nearly ten seconds. An ordinary race is what it looked to be.

Did that change in a hurry. In the last segment of the race, it appeared Elliott and Geoffrey Bodine, running abreast on the front row, touched slightly and slipped sideways between turns one and two. Dale Earnhardt darted under both, going in front to stay. Elliott would later charge that Earnhardt tagged Bodine, triggering the accident.

With seven laps to go, Elliott tried to overtake Earnhardt, swapping sheet metal with the leader in turn two and again in turn four. The latter bump sent Earnhardt slicing through the grass between the tri-oval homestretch and pit row. It seemed Earnhardt would lose traction and spin as grass flew, but he kept the car straight and angled back onto the pavement just short of the flag stand, still in front of Elliott. Earnhardt's save has gained fame in NASCAR lore as "The Pass in the Grass." That's catchy, but incorrect. He never lost the lead.

Before the bumping with Bill Elliott began, Dale Earnhardt (3) moved past fellow Chevrolet drivers Tim Richmond (25) and Harry Gant to find open track space and move to the head of the pack.

Earnhardt holds onto lead

with "Pass in the Grass"

"When Bill put me in the grass, that upset me, like it would any normal person. So I carried him high in the third turn. But I never touched him. Bill just got hot and bothered because he had the race won before tangling with Bodine."

—DALE EARNHARDT

A lap later, Earnhardt and Elliott touched again in turn three. Elliott said this impact cut his left rear tire, and he fell back to finish fourteenth, a lap down. Earnhardt was unchallenged the rest of the way, finishing .74 seconds ahead of runner-up Terry Labonte.

The fireworks weren't over. After the checkered flag, Elliott drove into Earnhardt on the backstretch, then swerved into him again on pit row.

"Earnhardt knew I had the best car and he cut me off from getting around him," said Elliott.

The first thing Earnhardt did upon arriving in the press box for the winner's interview—accompanied by burly bodyguards—was rush to check a video of the final ten laps.

"I know what happened out there," he said. "I'm just confirming it. . . . On the restart Bodine chopped Elliott off. . . . It was just reflexes that allowed me to get under 'em. . . . When Elliott knocked me into the grass, that got me hot. . . . I'm lucky the car came around straight."

Elliott also came to the press box after Earnhardt departed.

"Earnhardt hit Bodine and got him into me," charged a red-faced Elliott. "Dale later cut me off twice and he carried me up to the wall. . . ."

NASCAR moved quickly to defuse the situation, fining Elliott and Earnhardt $2,500 and ordering them to post $7,500 bonds against further mischief. Bodine was fined $1,000 and also had to post a $4,000 bond.

Governor Joe Frank Harris of Elliott's native Georgia phoned the Charlotte speedway during the week between The Winston and the track's Coca-Cola 600. He and other citizens of the state had raised the money to pay Elliott's fine.

Dale Earnhardt and his wife Teresa pose with The Winston trophy while an angered Bill Elliott, opposite, discusses his version of the finish with the assembled media.

1987 THE WINSTON
MAY 17, 1987
CHARLOTTE MOTOR SPEEDWAY
CONCORD, NORTH CAROLINA
1.5-MILE BANKED TRI-OVAL SUPERSPEEDWAY

Place	Driver	Make	Laps	Money	Pole Pos.
1.	Dale Earnhardt	Chev.	135	$200,000	4
2.	Terry Labonte	Chev.	135	$50,000	12
3.	Tim Richmond	Chev.	135	$40,000	2
4.	Geoffrey Bodine	Chev.	135	$30,000	5
5.	Rusty Wallace	Pont.	135	$19,000	7
6.	Kyle Petty	Ford	135	$14,000	15
7.	Morgan Shepherd	Buick	135	$12,000	17
8.	Bobby Allison	Buick	135	$11,400	14
9.	Darrell Waltrip	Chev.	135	$11,250	9
10.	Benny Parsons	Olds.	135	$10,900	6

Time of Race: 1 hour, 19 minutes, 24 seconds (run in three segments)
Average Speed: 53.023 mph
Margin of Victory: 0.74 seconds

1980
Winston 500

"I remember the crew kept telling me,
'Buddy's gaining,
Buddy's gaining.'
Well, he gained right past me."

—DALE EARNHARDT

After the 1980 Winston 500, it was clear that driver Buddy Baker was emotionally spent. But that's understandable considering the daunting odds he'd just beaten.

Big Buddy, in his vehicle nicknamed "the Gray Ghost" because it was so fast its paint scheme blended with the asphalt racing surface, and Dale Earnhardt, a young driver voted Rookie of the Year the previous season, were neck and neck when they both pitted for fuel and fresh tires on the 153rd of the race's 188 laps. Earnhardt's crew opted to change only the right side tires. Crew chief Waddell Wilson ordered four new tires for Baker.

"I've never worked on a car in which a driver was hurt," said the no-nonsense Wilson. "I wasn't about to see that change. We were wearing tires and had to have four new ones. That was it."

As a result, Baker came back on the track sixteen seconds behind leader Earnhardt, a huge margin on the 2.66-mile track that in later years became known as Talladega Superspeedway. However, Baker had a strong machine as he began a motoring mission to catch up. Baker was without radio communication as the race wound down. But the fans' excitement in the grandstands indicated to him that he was reeling Earnhardt in.

Baker stalks Earnhardt in

NASCAR

22 GREATEST RACES

Buddy Baker (28) leads
Dale Earnhardt (2) and Neil
Bonnett (on the inside) to the
tri-oval early in the race.

"That's the way you like winning races. Charging from behind. I always had a warm spot for this race because each lap we made up some ground until we were right there for the finish."** —BUDDY BAKER

charge from behind

"Sure, we lost some time and positions on the track. But getting four tires on that last pit stop wasn't a gamble.

We had the best car and driver on the track that day."

—WADDELL WILSON, CREW CHIEF FOR BUDDY BAKER

Buddy Baker (right) celebrates the victory with the man who gave him the horsepower: crew chief and engine builder Waddell Wilson.

"I drafted every car in sight," said Baker, considered a master of the aerodynamic phenomenon. "I even looked way ahead for slow cars so I could use their slipstream when I got within range."

Praised a rival, "Buddy Baker could get a boost off the air from a hot dog wrapper."

Baker steadily cut into Earnhardt's advantage. On lap 185 Baker was right on Earnhardt's bumper and on 186 he swept around the 1979 Rookie of the Year in turn three. Earnhardt made a spirited slingshot attempt to regain the lead but barely fell short. Baker's blistering stretch run was clocked at 202 mph and his winning margin was only three feet.

"This is as emotional a finish as I've ever had," said the veteran Baker. "I had all that catching up to do and it really tensed me. I'm so tickled I've been kissing my crew guys, even Buck Brigance [former motorcycle racing champion]."

Said Earnhardt, "The only way it could have been more exciting for me is to have won. I was going to give Buddy a shot down the backstretch the final lap, but couldn't because of a slower car. I wanted to be in the lead off turn four and make Buddy try to go around me in the tri-oval, but I couldn't swing that. He just overpowered us at the end."

Baker had complimentary words for Earnhardt. "That young man is going to be something else," he said of the driver destined to win seven NASCAR Winston Cup Series championships, the first coming later in 1980. "I'm lucky to have caught him here as a cub."

Harry Ranier's crew makes a four-tire stop on Buddy Baker's Oldsmobile, below. Baker was able to overcome a sixteen-second deficit in the final thirty-three laps to beat Dale Earnhardt by three feet.

1980 WINSTON 500
MAY 4, 1980
ALABAMA INTERNATIONAL MOTOR SPEEDWAY
TALLADEGA, ALABAMA
2.66-MILE BANKED TRI-OVAL SUPERSPEEDWAY

Place	Driver	Make	Laps	Money	Pole Pos.
1.	Buddy Baker	Olds.	188	$32,150	2
2.	Dale Earnhardt	Olds.	188	$28,700	4
3.	David Pearson	Olds.	188	$23,150	1
4.	Lennie Pond	Olds.	187	$20,500	7
5.	Tighe Scott	Olds.	186	$19,200	9
6.	Cale Yarborough	Olds.	186	$14,300	3
7.	Lake Speed	Chev.	185	$8,875	20
8.	Benny Parsons	Olds.	185	$11,750	8
9.	Dick Brooks	Olds.	184	$8,350	31
10.	Jody Ridley	Merc.	183	$9,185	17

Time of Race:	2 hours, 56 minutes, 0 seconds
Average Speed:	170.481 mph
Margin of Victory:	3 feet
Pole Winner:	David Pearson, 197.704 mph

1974 Firecracker 400

*"At the time, **I was really mad.** But the longer we get away from it, the better David's move looks. I wish I had thought of it."*—RICHARD PETTY

Driver David Pearson, nicknamed "the Fox" because of his cunning on the track, made an especially sly move to edge archrival Richard Petty for a controversial Firecracker 400 victory. Pearson had a "problem" going into the 160th and final lap at the sprawling 2.5-mile speedway: He was leading.

"The place to be on the last lap is running second just behind the leader," said Pearson, explaining his strategy on July 4, 1974. "This makes the leader real vulnerable for the following driver to use aerodynamics—the slingshot technique—to regain the lead with time running out."

So as he was racing through the tri-oval homestretch, Pearson eased off the gas pedal and guided his car slightly to the left about five hundred feet past the flag stand. Petty zoomed by, thinking Pearson's car was out of gas. Then Petty saw in his rearview mirror that Pearson was coming on fast from about a hundred yards behind.

Pearson pulled within a few feet of Petty's rear bumper through the banking of turns three and four, then whipped into the lead in the last thousand yards to take the checkered flag.

"Pearson usually drives a safer and saner race," a bristling Petty said immediately after alighting from his

Pearson fakes empty tank

"I think he was upset because he didn't think of it first."

—DAVID PEARSON

Richard Petty (43) stalks David Pearson (21) from the favored second position late in the 1974 Firecracker 400 at Daytona. Petty was preparing to slingshot past Pearson out of the draft and claim victory when the the Fox outsmarted the King.

to beat out Petty

1974 FIRECRACKER 400 JULY 4, 1974 DAYTONA INTERNATIONAL SPEEDWAY DAYTONA BEACH, FLORIDA 2.5-MILE BANKED TRI-OVAL SUPERSPEEDWAY				
Place Driver	Make	Laps	Money	Pole Pos.
1. David Pearson	Merc.	160	$17,350	1
2. Richard Petty	Dodge	160	$12,825	6
3. Buddy Baker	Ford	160	$12,237	5
(tie) Cale Yarborough	Chev.	160	$12,187	1
5. Bobby Allison	Mata.	159	$4,100	2
6. Bobby Isaac	Chev.	159	$1,900	7
7. Lennie Pond	Chev.	158	$3,450	19
8. Jackie Rogers	Chev.	157	$2,200	20
9. David Sisco	Chev.	155	$2,625	23
10. Cecil Gordon	Chev.	153	$2,000	32

Time of Race:	2 hours, 53 minutes, 32 seconds
Average Speed:	138.301 mph
Margin of Victory:	1 car length
Pole Winner:	David Pearson, 180.759 mph

car. "I could have hit him and wrecked us both going over 180 miles an hour."

Countered Pearson, "It wasn't a risky move where I made it."

Petty was so upset that he came to the press box to face Pearson, who was involved in the winner's postrace interview. Voices weren't raised in the exchange, but anger was evident nonetheless. The conversation went like this:

Petty: "It was real, real lucky I missed you and didn't crash both of us. It was close. It was a dangerous move. It scared me. . . . You didn't need to do it. There's no way I could have won the race. You were much faster than me."

Pearson: "Notice where I did it. I made sure we were out of the dogleg and heading straight. Where I did it, it wasn't a risky move. . . . Faster? I had tried to run off and I couldn't leave you. But you never would pass me, so I got all the way out of the throttle. I knew I had to be second the last lap to have a chance to win. I couldn't have won if I had stayed in front."

Pearson broke off the conversation at this point and left to join a group of waiting fans. But Petty had more to say. "If I had wanted to be a bad guy, I could have run him into the grass as we came to the flag. But I left him the lower lane, not the apron, a racing lane. I tried to take up as much room as possible and still be sanitary. . . . If I hadn't, our cars could have crashed and we'd have been in real trouble. . . . It's no big deal to be outrun. I'm not trying to persecute anyone, but a deal like this upsets you."

David Pearson's crew races to complete a two-tire change under the green flag, left. Below: Pearson and co-crew chief Leonard Wood celebrate Pearson's strategy of flipping off the ignition to make Petty believe his engine had failed.

Amazing

Aftermaths

Sometimes it's what happens after the race that is remembered

1979 Daytona 500

"The 1979 Daytona 500 humanized stock car racing for millions of Americans who before had seen only cars. **The raw emotions of the moment struck a chord with fans of every sport."**

—CBS COMMENTATOR KEN SQUIER

Television viewers across the country—many of them snowed in by a February blizzard—were treated to not only an exciting finish to the first flag-to-flag televised NASCAR race but also a spirited postrace fistfight. And NASCAR was treated to a massive, captive audience who would be thrilled by this dramatic introduction to the stock car racing organization.

The Daytona 500 progressed uneventfully enough during the first part of the race. But during the final thirty miles, drivers Donnie Allison and Cale Yarborough engaged in a tense two-driver duel after making up lost laps. Richard Petty, running third, was nineteen seconds behind the pair.

Starting the two-hundredth and final lap, Donnie Allison led with Yarborough only inches behind, positioned to make a slingshot pass along the backstretch of the 2.5-mile track. Halfway down the straightaway, Yarborough darted inside. Donnie moved left to block the challenge. Suddenly the two, racing abreast, smacked sheet metal and Yarborough was in the grass. They hit again as Yarborough drove back onto the asphalt, then hit again and angled sharply up the third turn banking and hard into the wall.

Petty, followed immediately by Darrell Waltrip and A. J. Foyt, was so far behind in turn two that he couldn't see the leaders collide.

Petty rides to victory as

Allisons, Yarborough duke it out

"They showed the whole race
—not just highlights between a Harlem Globetrotters 'game' and ice skating. I thought, 'It doesn't get any better than this.'"

—NASCAR FAN STEPHANIE CORCORAN, CLAYTON, OHIO

"I saw the yellow light flash on showing that something had happened," said Petty. "Knowing Donnie and Cale and how competitive they are, I figured it involved them."

Petty's car had been balky much of the race and he fretted about being overtaken in the final mile. Taking a low line the rest of the way around, Petty thwarted Waltrip's bid to pass in the tri-oval and won by a car length.

"It turns out Darrell's car was running as bad as mine—Darrell was on seven cylinders—so he couldn't come at me real hard," said Petty. "And A. J., well it appeared he eased off the throttle a bit when the yellow light came on, and this dropped him back a little too far to catch me."

As Petty took the checkered flag, CBS anchorman Ken Squier shouted, "There's a fight in turn three!"

The cameras then briefly showed Yarborough and the Allisons going at each other on the third turn apron, where the wrecked cars stopped. Blows and kicks were exchanged and Donnie swung his helmet.

"As I came around after the race ended it looked like Saturday night at a quarter-mile track in the old days," said an amused Petty.

Yarborough had popped from his car and angrily approached Donnie, pointing and shouting. At this time Bobby Allison arrived on the scene and stopped to check on his brother. Yarborough punched Bobby through the window screen of his car.

"I knew I had to do something about it right then or Cale would try to intimidate me from then on," said Bobby. "So I got out and all of a sudden Cale's nose was pounding on my fist."

Track workers quickly separated the three and broke up the melee.

"It's the worst thing I've ever seen," said a fuming Yarborough. "I had Donnie set up perfectly and he knew it. He put me in the grass. He knew he couldn't beat me any other way."

Countered Donnie, "Cale had made up his mind he was going to pass me low. I had made up my mind that if he was going to pass me at all, it was going to be high. When he went low, he went off the track, lost control, and hit me."

NASCAR president Bill France Jr. sternly admonished all three drivers and put Donnie Allison on probation. In retrospect he should have given them medals: The Daytona 500 of 1979 and its spirited ending is generally credited with igniting NASCAR's boom in growth and popularity.

As former leaders Donnie Allison and Cale Yarborough battled in the infield, Richard Petty (43) led Darrell Waltrip (88) to the flag to win the 1979 Daytona 500, left. Below: The Petty Enterprises crew kept Richard in contention with quick pits.

1979 DAYTONA 500

FEBRUARY 18, 1979
DAYTONA INTERNATIONAL SPEEDWAY
DAYTONA BEACH, FLORIDA
2.5-MILE BANKED TRI-OVAL SUPERSPEEDWAY

Place	Driver	Make	Laps	Money	Pole Pos.
1.	Richard Petty	Olds.	200	$73,900	13
2.	Darrell Waltrip	Olds.	200	$59,350	4
3.	A. J. Foyt	Olds.	200	$38,550	6
4.	Donnie Allison	Olds.	199	$39,600	2
5.	Cale Yarborough	Olds.	199	$34,525	3
6.	Tighe Scott	Buick	199	$24,550	33
7.	Chuck Bown	Buick	199	$18,895	28
8.	Dale Earnhardt	Buick	199	$22,845	10
9.	Coo Coo Marlin	Chev.	198	$15,885	37
10.	Frank Warren	Dodge	179	$17,475	24

Time of Race:	3 hours, 28 minutes, 22 seconds
Average Speed:	143.977 mph
Margin of Victory:	1 car length
Pole Winner:	Buddy Baker, Olds., 196.049 mph

"That win was always special to me . . . . It had been a long winter and I had all these doctors telling me I shouldn't race. They were probably right, but **I'm not giving that win back."**

—DRIVER RICHARD PETTY, WHO HAD UNDERGONE SURGERY TO REMOVE 40 PERCENT OF HIS STOMACH DURING THE OFF-SEASON

R

Richard Petty celebrates the sixth of his record seven Daytona 500 victories with his family, including then eighteen-year-old son Kyle (right).

David Pearson (21) and Gary Ballough (87) were among four cars eliminated in an accident on the fifty-third lap, top, although Bruce Hill (50) continued on and finished nineteenth. But the most memorable scene from the race was that of Cale Yarborough (center, holding helmet) battling the Allison brothers, Donnie (background) and Bobby (grabbing Yarborough's leg), after the last-lap accident. Track workers had to break up the fight.

1988

Checker 500

*"I just have a feeling. **Tomorrow I'm going to win my first race.** I've never won and I'm starting twenty-first. But I've got this feeling tomorrow is the day."*

—ALAN KULWICKI ON THE EVE OF HIS FIRST
NASCAR WINSTON CUP SERIES WIN AT PHOENIX

"I had been thinking for a couple months what I could do special when I finally won a race," said driver Alan Kulwicki after his triumphant first NASCAR Winston Cup Series win. "There'll never be another first win and I wanted to do something other than spewing champagne or standing on top of the car.

"I wanted to give the fans something to remember me and my first win by. I figured this would do it."

After winning the inaugural NASCAR Winston Cup Series event in Arizona, Kulwicki joined a breed that had become a rarity in NASCAR's so-called modern era dating to 1972: a driver who won in cars he owned and fielded himself. Kulwicki took the lead on the 297th of the race's 312 laps after the radiator hose broke in the dominant Buick of Ricky Rudd. When the trouble hit, Rudd was five seconds ahead after leading 182 laps on the flat one-mile oval track in the desert. Fighting back tears of elation, Kulwicki controlled his emotions long enough to drive his Ford to an 18.5-second victory in the five-hundred-kilometer event.

Kulwicki celebrates first

Perhaps the most unusual seats for a NASCAR Winston Cup Series race are on the hill overlooking turn four at Phoenix International Raceway. Fans carry everything from coolers to lawn chairs to canopy tents up the hill to get a panoramic view of the Checker 500, the track, the surrounding Arizona desert, and distant mountains.

win with "Polish victory lap"

Alan Kulwicki, shown below (in the Zerex Ford Thunderbird) beating the pack out of the pits under one of the six cautions, moved from twenty-first on the grid into the lead in only forty-six laps. The Phoenix International Raceway grandstand was packed to the rafters for the inaugural NASCAR Winston Cup event.

After taking the checkered flag, Kulwicki stunned spectators, the press corps, rival drivers, and crews by making a sudden U-turn in the fourth turn and heading back around the track in a counterclockwise direction. All the while he was waving in delight. "It was my Polish victory lap!" a beaming Kulwicki, whose ancestors were from Poland, shortly explained. His "reverse victory lap" has been repeated many times by other drivers.

Except for luck—two cases of good for Kulwicki, one case of bad for Rudd—Phoenix fans might never have seen the "Wrong Way Alan" stunt. Early in the race a lug nut rounded off during a change of Kulwicki's right rear tire. He narrowly averted losing a lap. "The crew couldn't get the tire off," said Kulwicki. "So I went with three new ones and the old one. I told the crew over the radio to get a six-point hand socket to twist the lug nut off during a later stop, and that worked."

Shortly afterward, as the field formed for a restart following a caution period,

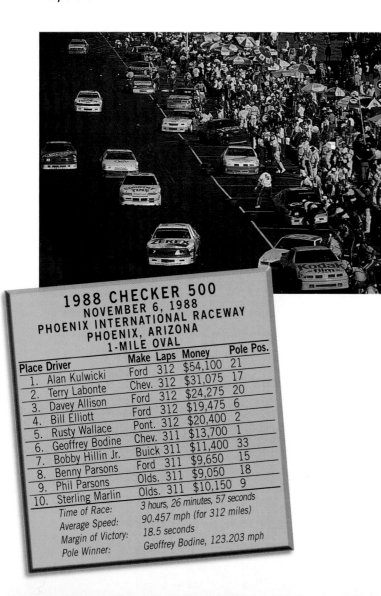

1988 CHECKER 500				
NOVEMBER 6, 1988				
PHOENIX INTERNATIONAL RACEWAY				
PHOENIX, ARIZONA				
1-MILE OVAL				
Place Driver	Make	Laps	Money	Pole Pos.
1. Alan Kulwicki	Ford	312	$54,100	21
2. Terry Labonte	Chev.	312	$31,075	17
3. Davey Allison	Ford	312	$24,275	20
4. Bill Elliott	Ford	312	$19,475	6
5. Rusty Wallace	Pont.	312	$20,400	2
6. Geoffrey Bodine	Chev.	311	$13,700	1
7. Bobby Hillin Jr.	Buick	311	$11,400	33
8. Benny Parsons	Ford	311	$9,650	15
9. Phil Parsons	Olds.	311	$9,050	18
10. Sterling Marlin	Olds.	311	$10,150	9

Time of Race:	3 hours, 26 minutes, 57 seconds
Average Speed:	90.457 mph (for 312 miles)
Margin of Victory:	18.5 seconds
Pole Winner:	Geoffrey Bodine, 123.203 mph

the right front tire was going flat on Kulwicki's car. Rival Terry Labonte happened to notice. "Terry radioed his crew guys and they relayed word to us," said Paul Andrews, Kulwicki's crew chief. "We were really fortunate." Ironically, Labonte was to finish as runner-up in the race.

Perhaps the most pivotal development to the outcome occurred when Rudd suddenly slowed in the car that looked unbeatable. "The tach started acting crazy," said Rudd. "The temperature gauge did the same. I backed off and tried to nurse the car along, but the engine blew anyway." This put Kulwicki in front and set him to fighting his emotions in order to stay focused.

"I was almost crying the last few laps," said Kulwicki, the fourth first-time winner in 1988 and the circuit's record fourteenth different victor. "It has been a long road with a lot of heartache since I came from Wisconsin to North Carolina to join the Winston Cup tour in 1985. But this makes it all worthwhile."

"I think it's great for the sport that someone like Kulwicki can come in here on his own and build a winning car. I salute him. He's climbed our Mount Everest."

—BENNY PARSONS

1995
Goody's 500

> *"This is a stand-up-and-be counted sport.* There are times you listen. And there are times when you have to make yourself heard. I wasn't going to stay mad at Dale. But I needed to have him know how I felt at that moment."
>
> —RUSTY WALLACE

It looked like a hokey Hollywood movie about auto racing, only this time the action was real, including two superstar drivers jaw to jaw in an angry post-race confrontation. The two were Dale Earnhardt and Rusty Wallace. Early in the 1995 Goody's 500 at Bristol Motor Speedway, a bump from Earnhardt caused Wallace to spin out.

Wallace became so angry while accosting Earnhardt afterward that he hurled a plastic water bottle at the Intimidator. Less angry was Terry Labonte, who managed to drive his mangled car to victory lane after spinning across the finish line in a shower of sparks from a bump by onrushing Earnhardt.

Labonte hit the wall after bouncing off the lapped car of Greg Sacks, heavily damaging the winning Chevrolet as it took the flag. "I'm not mad," said Labonte, nicknamed "the Iceman" because of his calm demeanor. "If I hadn't won I might be mad. I don't think Dale tried to wreck me. We just got caught in slower traffic at the end of the

Labonte spins spectacularly across

Night racing at Bristol, Tennessee, provided such spectacular images as the late-race battle between eventual winner Terry Labonte (5) and Mark Martin (6). Labonte passed Martin to the high side en route to the front of the pack.

"Did I expect to get bumped at the finish line? All that was between Dale Earnhardt and the checkered flag was my car."

—TERRY LABONTE

finish line in shower of sparks

race and it created a tight situation. I knew he was coming on real fast.

"Dale gave me a shot in the back and I just stood on the gas and held on. Dale's bump knocked me off the slower car on the inside of the track. Luckily I was able to keep the wheels pointed in the right direction long enough to get to the line."

Early in the race Earnhardt was ordered to the back by NASCAR officials as a penalty for the contact with the strong-running car of Wallace on the thirty-second of the race's five hundred laps at the .533-mile track. Wallace wound up finishing twenty-first and sought out Earnhardt after the race to confront him on the contact.

"Rusty, we need to talk," replied Earnhardt. "I didn't do it on purpose. It was just close racing."

But Wallace wasn't mollified. He let the water bottle fly. It bounced off the roof of Earnhardt's car and lightly hit the many-time champion in the nose.

Thirty-six hours later Wallace gracefully moved to defuse the situation. "It's amazing how you can wake up the next morning and not be as mad. . . . Dale and I are friends, and we'll always be friends," said Wallace.

Nevertheless, the plastic water bottle already had sailed into NASCAR lore, and longtime followers of stock car racing were chuckling about how lucky Earnhardt was.

In the old days, they observed, the water bottle likely would have been a tire tool.

Lake Speed's crew burns the midnight oil, opposite top, making repairs to the Ford Thunderbird following an accident. The efforts were to no avail and Speed was forced to retire after completing 391 of the 500 laps.

Opposite bottom: Dale Earnhardt (3) moves to the inside to put Rusty Wallace another lap down late in the race.

1995 GOODY'S 500
AUGUST 26, 1995
BRISTOL MOTOR SPEEDWAY
BRISTOL, TENNESSEE
.533-MILE PAVED OVAL

Place	Driver	Make	Laps	Money	Pole Pos.
1.	Terry Labonte	Chev.	500	$66,940	2
2.	Dale Earnhardt	Chev.	500	$65,890	7
3.	Dale Jarrett	Ford	500	$39,390	16
4.	Darrell Waltrip	Chev.	500	$32,780	20
5.	Mark Martin	Ford	500	$41,775	1
6.	Jeff Gordon	Chev.	500	$27,865	4
7.	Sterling Marlin	Chev.	500	$26,140	19
8.	Mike Wallace	Ford	500	$14,840	27
9.	Jeff Burton	Ford	500	$22,515	18
10.	Derrike Cope	Ford	499	$20,565	10

Time of Race:	3 hours, 15 minutes, 3 seconds
Average Speed:	81.979 mph
Margin of Victory:	.10-second
Pole Winner:	Mark Martin, 125.093 mph (track record)

"I am amazed by the skill and killer instinct Dale exhibited."

—NASCAR FAN FRANNA L. HOWARD, HOUSTON, TEXAS

1992 The Winston

"What hurt most the morning after was the fact that I crushed that car."

—DAVEY ALLISON, WHOSE SPIN AFTER WINNING THE WINSTON DESTROYED A THUNDERBIRD THAT HAD FOUR WINS AND A SECOND IN FIVE CHARLOTTE STARTS

K Kyle Petty appeared to have the 1992 Winston All-Star race victory in hand after leader Dale Earnhardt spun in turn four on the final frantic lap. But then Davey Allison closed fast down the homestretch, whipping to the inside and scraping metal with Petty's Pontiac as Allison charged to The Winston's checkered flag. The late pass gave Allison his second straight win in the all-star race.

Thunderous cheering erupted from the 133,500 spectators—the largest crowd at that time to witness a nighttime sports event in the United States. But then the applause turned to silence as Allison spun just a few feet past the flag stand and careened down the track, hitting the wall.

"We hit before we got to the flag stand, then rubbed again after crossing the line," said Petty. "It was unintentional. We were both out of control and leaning on each other. Davey came across and clipped my left front, and that got him sideways.

"Just before that, Dale and I had a bad angle going into the third turn. I knew we weren't going to make it all the way through that end of the speedway without trouble. When Dale's car got away from him, I had to ease up a little. But Davey was able to hold his line and

Davey Allison spins past

Davey Allison (inside) and
Rusty Wallace bring the field
toward the start of The Winston
at Charlotte Motor Speedway in
1992. Bill Elliott is on the
inside of the second row with
Ken Schrader to his right.

finish line for the win

Place	Driver	Make	Laps	Money	Pole Pos.
1.	Davey Allison	Ford	70	$300,000	1
2.	Kyle Petty	Pont.	70	$130,000	16
3.	Ken Schrader	Chev.	70	$50,000	4
4.	Ricky Rudd	Chev.	70	$30,000	9
5.	Bill Elliott	Ford	70	$47,000	3
6.	Rusty Wallace	Pont.	70	$42,500	2
7.	Alan Kulwicki	Ford	70	$23,000	14
8.	Ernie Irvan	Chev.	70	$31,500	17
9.	Richard Petty	Pont.	70	$20,500	15
10.	Terry Labonte	Chev.	70	$19,500	13

1992 THE WINSTON
MAY 16, 1992
CHARLOTTE MOTOR SPEEDWAY
CONCORD, NORTH CAROLINA
1.5-MILE BANKED TRI-OVAL SUPERSPEEDWAY

Time of Race: 47 minutes, 29 seconds
Average Speed: 132.678 mph
Margin of Victory: 2 feet
Pole Winner: Davey Allison, 135.265 mph

maintain his speed. My only hope was to block him."

He was taken to the track's infield care center. Videotapes appeared to show Allison smiling wanly and waving to fans as he was put in the ambulance the night of May 16, 1992.

The popular driver later was transported to a hospital where it was determined he had sustained serious bruises and a concussion. Allison was released the next day and competed in the speedway's Coca-Cola 600 the following weekend.

"Davey got his bell rung, but because NASCAR is so strict about safety in the cars, he is going to be okay," said crew chief Larry McReynolds.

Allison was unaware he had won until visited by McReynolds and team owner Robert Yates in the infirmary.

"What happened?" Allison asked.

"We won!" replied Yates.

Allison thrust a clenched fist into the air.

Petty came to the press box for the postrace interview because Allison couldn't.

"I hate I'm up here and Davey isn't," said Petty. "I don't like to be involved in wrecks."

"There are no hard feelings," assured Yates. "It was just close racing."

A grinning Earnhardt had embraced Petty in the garage area immediately after the race. "Kyle was just trying to take what was his," said Earnhardt, the only other two-time winner of The Winston. "This is a glamorous race and he was going for it."

Allison won $300,000 but lamented destroying his Ford Thunderbird, nicknamed "007." He had driven the car to an amazing record at the Charlotte track, four victories and a runner-up finish in five starts.

Davey Allison, opposite, referred to his first-to-third final lap sprint under the spinning Dale Earnhardt and past Kyle Petty as "the best single lap" of his career. Below: Jarrett's smoking Chevrolet rolls to a stop after an accident on the twelfth lap of The Winston. Jarrett was unable to continue.

Finally!

The culmination of lifelong struggles played out on the racetrack

1998 Daytona 500

> ## "So close, so close so many times
> ### and nothing. The first times you just miss, you think next year. But you really start to wonder. Which is why this is so darn great."
>
> —DALE EARNHARDT

For two decades Dale Earnhardt had been asked the nettlesome question over and over and over again:

"When are you going to win the Daytona 500?"

Among NASCAR's major events, only the five-hundred-miler at Daytona International Speedway, the biggest, most glamorous NASCAR Winston Cup Series race, had eluded the driver many fans rate the best of all time. It wasn't that Earnhardt couldn't perform at Daytona. He listed thirty victories at the track in other races, by far the best record of anyone. He just seemed jinxed in the 500, once losing when he cut a tire while leading only a mile from the finish line.

Three other times he had led going into the last ten laps, only to lose.

Finally, on February 15, 1998, Earnhardt had the long-awaited answer to The Big Question: Now.

Earnhardt erased two decades of February frustration at Daytona, and also snapped a fifty-nine-race streak without a victory by scoring a heart-pounding triumph. Flashing the aggressive, charging style that made him a seven-time NASCAR Winston Cup Series champion, Earnhardt remained in strong contention throughout the race. On the 179th of the race's 200 laps he assumed the lead for the fourth time, passing teammate Mike Skinner in the fourth turn.

After twenty years Earnhardt

A jubilant Dale Earnhardt gives a victory wave as he takes the checkered flag on his first Daytona 500 win. Following Earnhardt to the finish was runner-up Bobby Labonte and (to the inside) the lapped car of Rick Mast.

gets his Daytona 500

"He won the Daytona 500 the way Dale Earnhardt should win the Daytona 500. **He dominated.**"

—BILL ELLIOTT

Earnhardt remained in front as the laps wound down and the mounting tension became so unbearable for some fans that they wept and hid their faces, unable to watch. Bobby Labonte was coming on strong. Could he overtake and pass Earnhardt, denying the Intimidator yet again? On the 199th lap, drivers Jimmy Spencer and John Andretti collided in the second turn, forcing a yellow flag. If Earnhardt could stay ahead and make it back to the flag stand to take the caution first, victory was his.

Earnhardt made it a couple car lengths ahead of Labonte, setting off a wild celebration among the Earnhardt crew and thousands of spectators.

Normally cool Danny "Chocolate" Myers of Earnhardt's Richard Childress–owned team grabbed everyone he could reach. Shaking them, the hulking Myers screamed, "He did it! He did it! Oh, God."

Earnhardt, grinning widely beneath his wraparound reflective sunglasses, said, "I cried a little bit in the race car on the way to the checkered flag . . . well, maybe not cried, but my eyes watered up.

"What I was hoping was that the other drivers would stay in line until five laps to go then they'd start racing each other behind me. That happened and it made me feel better. . . . It was my time, I guess. I've been passed on the last lap, run out of gas, and cut a tire. . . . I don't care how we won it, but we won it."

As Earnhardt drove down pit row a remarkable thing happened: Hundreds of crewmen from rival teams lined the route to touch his hand, and Earnhardt accommodated them by inching along. After clearing the crowd, Earnhardt drove onto the grass near the flag stand and, gassing the engine, cut several "donuts" in the sod.

Arriving in the press box for an interview that seemed more like a coronation, Earnhardt pulled a stuffed monkey from his driving uniform and slammed it down. "I'm here, and I've got that damned monkey off my back!" he proclaimed.

While Earnhardt answered questions in the tower, far below fans were taking pieces of the turf as mementoes. Some fans lay in the tire tracks. Several aligned themselves to form his car's number, creating a human 3.

Earnhardt looked down on all this and said, "Race fans are awesome. . . . Gosh it's a great day."

Dale Earnhardt was seemingly even more focused than ever leading up to the fortieth Daytona 500. Although he had won thirty other races at the track, he was zero for nineteen in NASCAR's premier event. Below: The Richard Childress crew provided Earnhardt with flawless pit stops throughout the afternoon.

	1998 DAYTONA 500					
	FEBRUARY 15, 1998					
	DAYTONA INTERNATIONAL SPEEDWAY					
	DAYTONA BEACH, FLORIDA					
	2.5-MILE BANKED TRI-OVAL SUPERSPEEDWAY					
Place	Driver	Make	Laps	Money		Pole Pos.
1.	Dale Earnhardt	Chev.	200	$1,059,805		4
2.	Bobby Labonte	Pont.	200	$549,255		1
3.	Jeremy Mayfield	Ford	200	$375,705		13
4.	Ken Schrader	Chev.	200	$313,480		31
5.	Rusty Wallace	Ford	200	$232,705		12
6.	Ernie Irvan	Pont.	200	$205,200		10
7.	Chad Little	Ford	200	$127,680		21
8.	Mike Skinner	Chev.	200	$135,705		8
9.	Michael Waltrip	Ford	200	$142,705		6
10.	Bill Elliott	Ford	200	$129,155		19

Time of Race:	2 hours, 53 minutes, 42 seconds
Average Speed:	172.712 mph
Margin of Victory:	Under caution
Pole Winner:	Bobby Labonte, 192.415 mph

In past Daytona 500s, Earnhardt, receiving a congratulatory handshake from Bill France, top left, and kiss from his wife and daughter, left, had been denied by his running low on gas, blown tires, late accidents, and a bird that flew into his Chevrolet.

After so many near misses, Dale Earnhardt celebrated by spinning donuts on the grass between Daytona International Speedway's tri-oval front straight and pit row before being mobbed by the press..

"If it couldn't be me, then let it be Dale. The Daytona 500 is our greatest race. It wouldn't have been right had a champion like Dale Earnhardt not enjoyed victory in this race."

—KEN SCHRADER

1989
Daytona 500

"The Good Lord wanted me to win this race. I believe that. How else can you explain the car running on fumes like that?"

—DARRELL WALTRIP

After sixteen starts at the Daytona 500 without a win, one might think Darrell Waltrip would be psychically out of gas. Waltrip had garnered other milestone triumphs at Darlington, Talladega, and Charlotte, but a victory in NASCAR Winston Cup Series' classic race had always eluded him. But in 1989 he easily mustered the strength, will, and courage to give it another go—it was his Chevy running out of gas he had to worry about.

With twenty laps to go on the 2.5-mile track, drafting partners Ken Schrader and Dale Earnhardt held a commanding 7.2-second lead. On lap 190, the two pitted together for fuel. Earnhardt's stop took only 4 seconds. Schrader, in for 6.2 seconds, was 3.52 seconds behind Earnhardt upon returning to the track.

The stops left Alan Kulwicki and Waltrip running 1-2. The duo stayed on the speedway, making no move toward pit row. On the 197th lap Kulwicki suddenly slowed in turn one as a tire went down. Waltrip zipped by to take first place.

Waltrip wins Daytona 500

Few drivers have ever had more fun celebrating a victory than Darrell Waltrip (left) did at the 1989 Daytona 500.

running on fumes

Darrell Waltrip was virtually out of gas as he took the checkered flag. Over the last couple laps, Waltrip (17) would weave back and forth, making sure the last gallons of fuel reached the pickup valve.

"I didn't think there was any way Darrell was going to **make it to the finish on the gas he had.** But he did. And that was the story."

—KEN SCHRADER, WALTRIP'S TEAMMATE

As Waltrip came back around, Hammond stepped across the pit wall, signaling his driver to come in. However, Waltrip had no intention of stopping even though repeatedly in the last three laps Waltrip thought his fuel cell had run dry.

"It's out! It's gone!" Waltrip shouted to his crew via radio. "The fuel pressure is zero. . . . Oh, no it's not! The fuel pressure has picked up. It's going again!"

Hammond screamed advice into his radio. "Shake it, baby! Shake it!" Hammond bellowed, meaning that Waltrip should zigzag in an effort to slosh what little fuel was left into the gas line.

"I think I can make it. . . . We might be able to. . . . We'll try it," Waltrip radioed breathlessly.

Schrader, so strong he'd led 114 laps, was coming on in a rush, easily passing Earnhardt for second place. The race was Schrader's if Waltrip was a drop or two short of the fuel he needed.

Waltrip wasn't.

"I knew we were in trouble with three laps to go," said Schrader with a sigh. "Darrell had been legging it [running conservatively] and I knew that was his strategy, to gamble on not making a late stop for gas."

"I sensed we were going to pull it off," said Waltrip, who ran the final fifty-three laps—or 132.5 miles—on twenty-two gallons of gas. "It's true that cars ordinarily get barely six miles per gallon here, but I drafted everything in sight. This let me roll out of the throttle and conserve fuel."

How much fuel was left in Waltrip's car at the end?

"So little it wouldn't fill a thimble," said a NASCAR inspector. "So little, that for $5 I'd drink it."

A midrace snarl in the pits caused Darrell Waltrip valuable time. Traffic caused Waltrip to stop wide of his stall, forcing his crewmen to travel an extra distance with the fuel and tires. As Waltrip's Chevrolet (17) is serviced, Geoffrey Bodine (5) and Brett Bodine (15) head back to the track.

"When the man sitting next to me said that he heard Darrell say on the scanner that he was going for it,
my heart skipped a beat."

—NASCAR FAN GREG BROWN, OWENSBORO, KENTUCKY

1989 DAYTONA 500
FEBRUARY 19, 1989
DAYTONA INTERNATIONAL SPEEDWAY
DAYTONA BEACH, FLORIDA
2.5-MILE BANKED TRI-OVAL SUPERSPEEDWAY

Place	Driver	Make	Laps	Money	Pole Pos.
1.	Darrell Waltrip	Chev.	200	$184,900	2
2.	Ken Schrader	Chev.	200	$182,700	1
3.	Dale Earnhardt	Chev.	200	$95,550	8
4.	Geoffrey Bodine	Chev.	200	$79,250	10
5.	Phil Parsons	Olds.	200	$70,325	7
6.	Rick Mast	Chev.	200	$52,525	11
7.	Alan Kulwicki	Ford	200	$52,325	9
8.	Rick Wilson	Olds.	200	$47,325	40
9.	Terry Labonte	Ford	200	$88,400	4
10.	Eddie Bierschwale	Ford	200	$31,725	41

Time of Race: 3 hours, 22 minutes, 4 seconds
Average Speed: 148.466 mph
Margin of Victory: 2.84 seconds
Pole Winner: Ken Schrader, 196.996 mph

Pepsi Firecracker 400

"I have seen a lot of strange finishes in my career, but **Greg Sacks' victory in 1985 had a lot of us shaking our heads."**

—KYLE PETTY

Greg Sacks' stunning victory in the Pepsi Firecracker 400 was characterized by experiment. Sacks' Chevrolet was a "research and development" vehicle. His team, Bill Gardner Racing, had been formed three weeks earlier under the guidance of engineer Gary Nelson. Some of his pickup pit crew had never been to a NASCAR Winston Cup Series race, or even met each other prior to this one—introductions were made in the pit that morning. But the biggest experiment of all for the dazed Sacks was becoming a NASCAR Winston Cup Series winner: The Long Island driver had trouble locating victory lane.

"Winning hasn't sunk in," said Sacks, who seemed in shock in victory lane. "It might take a day or two for the magnitude of this to hit me."

Gardner, who also owned the DiGard team of driver Bobby Allison, appeared shocked, too. First, a grinning Gardner said it "wasn't a wild dream" to think a patchwork team could win. Then he called the development "a Cinderella story."

It was the latter.

"The group we assembled in the pits was more a skeleton crew than a pickup crew," said Nelson, destined to become NASCAR Winston Cup Series director in later years. "Tony Price, who carried

R&D car gives Sacks

"... the second we hit the track, I knew we had a strong car. I never had so much fun. And then we won."

—GREG SACKS

Greg Sacks takes the checkered flag in his one-of-a-kind R&D Chevrolet to win the Pepsi Firecracker 400 at Daytona International Speedway on July 4, 1985. Sacks' only NASCAR Winston Cup Series victory remains one of the bigger upsets in NASCAR history.

one of NASCAR's biggest upsets

"That's one of those amazing stories that makes racing great."

—BILL ELLIOTT

the tires on pit stops, was hired just two weeks ago and sleeps in our shop. Robert Blestek [who scored two touchdowns in eighty-three seconds in 1983 as Boston College beat Alabama] would have been in an NFL tryout camp except for a broken arm.

"Most of our crewmen didn't know each other. They introduced themselves in the pits.

"As the race went on and Greg hung in there, I said to myself, 'Uh-oh, we're going to have to make some pit stops that are going to mean something.' I didn't think much of our chances." The crewmen did fine and Sacks, a Modified Division star in New England, sped to his first big-time victory. Going into the 400 he listed just two top-ten finishes in forty-one NASCAR Winston Cup Series starts, with a best of sixth in the 1985 Daytona 500.

During the last half of the 160-lap race at Daytona International Speedway, Sacks dueled tightly with prerace favorite Bill Elliott, but flashed to the finish line 23.98 seconds ahead. Runner-up Elliott fell far behind on lap 152 when he had to pit for enough fuel to finish the final twenty miles. Elliott's crew said a vibration shook loose his Ford's fuel pickup, enabling him to use only seventeen and a half of twenty-two gallons in the gasoline cell.

Sacks led thirty-three laps, including the final nine after Elliott pitted.

"Greg ran a good race, he deserved to win," said Elliott, who led 103 laps. "Toward the end he was really tough."

Sacks made a risky pass of Terry Labonte in turn four on the last lap. In another oddity, the radio in Sacks' helmet was out and he thought he was racing the lapped Labonte for the victory.

Of Sacks' triumph, Labonte spoke for many when he said, "I was surprised. I'm still surprised. I'll be surprised for a long time."

Greg Sacks passes to the inside to put Neil Bonnett a lap down late in the Pepsi Firecracker 400, opposite. Below: Sacks celebrates his amazing victory.

1985 PEPSI FIRECRACKER 400
JULY 4, 1985
DAYTONA INTERNATIONAL SPEEDWAY
DAYTONA BEACH, FLORIDA
2.5-MILE BANKED TRI-OVAL SUPERSPEEDWAY

Place	Driver	Make	Laps	Money	Pole Pos.
1.	Greg Sacks	Chev.	160	$45,350	9
2.	Bill Elliott	Ford	160	$41,800	1
3.	Darrell Waltrip	Chev.	160	$26,100	19
4.	Ron Bouchard	Buick	160	$16,730	13
5.	Kyle Petty	Ford	160	$15,570	10
6.	Buddy Baker	Olds.	160	$12,475	32
7.	Ricky Rudd	Ford	160	$14,500	3
8.	Terry Labonte	Chev.	159	$16,550	4
9.	Dale Earnhardt	Chev.	159	$13,400	18
10.	David Pearson	Chev.	159	$8,150	12

Time of Race: 2 hours, 31 minutes, 12 seconds
Average Speed: 158.730 mph
Margin of Victory: 23.98 seconds
Pole Winner: Bill Elliott, 201.523 mph

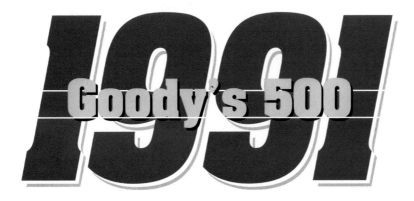

1991 Goody's 500

"Harry is something. He's a tough old guy. One thing is for sure, he's giving all of us a new lease on our careers. If we use him for an example, we should be getting faster around fifty."

—DALE EARNHARDT

Life begins at fifty-one.

At least it did for Harry Gant in September 1991 when he became the oldest driver to win a NASCAR Winston Cup race on four straight Sundays.

The four straight victories tied a modern NASCAR Winston Cup record. And the total was six straight wins if you included two victories in the NASCAR Busch Series, Grand National Division.

The streak was capped on September 22, 1991, in the Goody's 500 at Martinsville Speedway as Gant passed eleven cars in the final hundred laps after being nudged into the fourth-turn wall while dueling Rusty Wallace for the lead.

Gant had stretched the streak to three straight by winning despite spinning the previous Sunday at Dover, Delaware, where he swept the weekend's two races.

Now he was twelfth in line at Martinsville with just over fifty miles to run on the .526-mile bullring. His crew had patched the right front of his Oldsmobile with quick stops on three straight laps under the yellow.

Gant quickly started picking off the opposition until he came up on leader Brett Bodine with fifty-four laps to go. Gant took the lead. Bodine battled back. They dueled for eight laps until Gant took the lead for good.

Four straight at fifty-one.

"Harry Gant seemed to treat Martinsville as a quiet Sunday drive in the country."

—NASCAR FAN ROGER MORRIS,
WELDON, CALIFORNIA

1991 GOODY'S 500
SEPTEMBER 22, 1991
MARTINSVILLE SPEEDWAY
MARTINSVILLE, VIRGINIA
.526-MILE PAVED OVAL

Place	Driver	Make	Laps	Money	Pole Pos.
1.	Harry Gant	Olds.	500	$64,000	12
2.	Brett Bodine	Buick	500	$36,825	2
3.	Dale Earnhardt	Chev.	500	$30,350	5
4.	Ernie Irvan	Chev.	500	$19,300	13
5.	Mark Martin	Ford	500	$24,575	1

Time of Race: 3 hours, 31 minutes, 42 seconds
Average Speed: 74.535 mph
Margin of Victory: 1 second
Pole Winner: Mark Martin, 93.171 mph

Gant takes win record

Harry Gant (33) hugs the inside curb while fighting off Rusty Wallace's challenge for the lead midway through the Goody's 500 at Martinsville, Virginia. Gant led 226 of the 500 laps, including the final 46.

Using duct tape and metal shears, Harry Gant's crew needed only three yellow-flag pit stops to repair the damage to the right front of their Oldsmobile after a brush with the wall.

at age fifty-one

Special thanks to the many fans who took the time to rank NASCAR's greatest races online at www.NASCAR.com; to the drivers for their time and effort; and to the following motorsports writers for participating in the survey:

Mark Allen, Maverick Entertainment, Inc., Charlotte, North Carolina

Mark Armijo, *The Arizona Republic,* Phoenix, Arizona

Jeff Barnhart, *Denton Record-Chronicle,* Grapevine, Texas

Patrick Berger, Street and Smith's Productions, Charlotte, North Carolina

Dick Berggren, *American Stock Car Racing Magazine,* Ipswich, Massachusetts

Dan Bianchi, Auto Media Associates, Peekskill, New York

Dan Carney, *Autoweek,* Herndon, Virginia

Bill Center, *San Diego Union-Tribune,* San Diego, California

Michael Cercel, Sports Ticker, Jersey City, New Jersey

Bill Chipps, *IEG Sponsorship Report,* Chicago, Illinois

Bill Coats, *St. Louis Post-Dispatch,* St. Louis, Missouri

Tommy Dampier, *Lee Country Observer,* Bishopville, South Carolina

Tom Duffy, *National Speed Sport News,* Shadyside, Ohio

Stephanie Boyd Durner, *Inside NASCAR,* Charlotte, North Carolina

Monte Dutton, *Gaston Gazette,* Clinton, South Carolina

Mark Florence, *All About Cars,* Pittsville, Wisconsin

Jack Flowers, *Speedway Scene,* Charlotte, North Carolina

John Jay Fox, The Morning Call, Allentown, Pennsylvania

Norm Froscher, motorsports writer, Gainesville, Florida

Chris Gill, *The Leader,* Corning, New York

Walt Glatthaar, KMOX-CBS-Radio-Fox, Belleville, Illinois

Mike Griffith, *Knoxville News-Sentinel,* Daphne, Alabama

Mike Harris, Associated Press, Wake Forest, North Carolina

Jim Hawkins, *Oakland Press,* Commerce Township, Michigan

Mike Hembree, *Greenville News,* Spartanburg, South Carolina

Richard Huff, *New York Daily News,* Highlands, New Jersey

Godwin Kelly, *Daytona Beach News-Journal,* Palm Coast, Florida

Mike Kerchner, *National Speed Sport News,* Harrisburg, North Carolina

Bob Latford, Inside Line Newsletter, Concord, North Carolina

Ron Lemasters, Jr., *National Speed Sport News,* Harrisburg, North Carolina

Leon Mandel, *AutoWeek,* Detroit, Michigan

John Marcase, *The Town Talk,* Alexandria, Louisiana

Gary McCredie, *NASCAR Racing for Teens,* Concord, North Carolina

Sandra Mckee, *The Baltimore Sun,* Baltimore, Maryland

Jim McLaurin, *The State,* Elgin, South Carolina

Paul Melhado, *Circle Track Magazine,* Los Angeles, California

Charlie Mitchell, The Hour, Norwalk, Connecticut

Dick Mittman, Indianapolis Motor Speedway, Indianapolis, Indiana

Mike Owens, Fastrack Publishing, Gastonia, North Carolina

Caron Papas-Myers, Lazarus Productions, Inc., Lexington, North Carolina

Joseph Patrick, *Gater Racing Photo News,* Syracuse, New York

Tom Peterson, Knight Ridder/Tribune News Service, Washington D.C.

Pete Pistone, *Chicgo Sun-Times/* WGN Radio, Schaumburg, Illinois

Thomas Pope, *Fayetteville Observer-Times,* Fayetteville, North Carolina

Steve Post, *Gater Racing News,* Concord, North Carolina

Kay Presto, Presto Productions, Ontario, California

Dennis Punch, *The Speedway Report,* Newton, North Carolina

Pete Richards, TNN/RaceDay, Charlotte, North Carolina

Dave Rodman, NASCAR Online, Daytona Beach, Florida

Jack Rux, ANG Newspapers, Pleasanton, California

Ernie Saxton, *Times Herald,* Langhorne, Pennsylvania

Paul Schaefer, *NASCAR Magazine,* Daytona Beach, Florida

Jimmy Smothers, *The Gadsden Times,* Gadsden, Alabama

Mike Snow, *Speedway Scene,* Raleigh, North Carolina

Ken Squier, CBS Sports, Waterbury, Vermont

Bill Stephens, CBS Sports, Osterville, Maryland

Stan Sutton, *The Herald Times,* Bloomington, Indiana

Jeff Taylor, Pioneer Press Newspapers, Cary, Illinois

Tim Tuttle, *On Track Magazine,* Brownsburg, Indiana

Lori Vizza, *Speedway Scene,* Raleigh, North Carolina

Steve Waid, Street and Smith's Sports Group, Charlotte, North Carolina

Scott Walsh, *Scranton Times-Tribune,* Scranton, Pennsylvania

Tom Whitmore, Fastrack Publishing Co., Chester, Virginia

Dave Woolford, *Toledo Blade,* Toledo, Ohio

Eric Wright, Sponsors Report, Ann Arbor, Michigan

PHOTOGRAPHY CREDITS

Daytona Racing Archives: 5, 6, 8-9, 10-11, 12, 13, 14-15, 16, 17A and B, 18-19, 21, 22, 22-23, 24, 25A and B, 28, 29, 36, 37, 38-39, 40-41, 42, 43, 44-45, 46A and B, 46-47, 47B, 52, 53A, 55, 64-65, 66, 67, 68, 69, 70-71, 72, 73, 74, 74-75, 76, 82, 82-83, 84-85, 85, 86-87, 88-89, 90, 91A, B and C, 92A and B, 93, 94-95, 96, 97, 98-99, 101, 102-103, 104A and B, 106-107, 108-109, 110, 111, 112, 112-113, 113, 114, 114-115, 118, 118-119, 121A and B, 124, 125, 126-127, 128-129, 132-133, 134-135, 137, 138-139, 140, 141, 142, 143A and B.

The Daytona Beach *News-Journal:* 26-27.

Jim Fluharty: 50-51, 59A, 132, 132-133, 133

Painting by Buzz McKim: 62-63.

Dozier Mobley: 49, 53B, 100, 122-123.

Phoenix International Speedway/Warren Faidley: 116.

Phoenix International Speedway/T. Rempe: 116-117.

George Tiedemann: 2-3, 20, 23, 30-31, 32, 33, 34A and B, 35, 48, 56-57, 58, 58-59, 60, 60-61, 78, 78-79, 80, 81, 130, 131, 132B, 134, 136.